BIBLE ENGAGEMENT BASICS

Lawson W. Murray

Scripture Union

Bible Engagement Basics

Lawson W. Murray

Copyright © 2017 by **Scripture Union**

The printing of this copy has been provided by:

SU Scotland
70 Milton Street
Glasgow
G4 0HR

0141 332 1162
info@suscotland.org.uk
www.suscotland.org.uk

All Scripture quotations, unless otherwise indicated, are taken from The Holy Bible, New International Version®, NIV® Copyright © 1973, 1978, 1984, 2011 by Biblica, Inc.™ Used by permission. All rights reserved worldwide.

Book Layout © 2014 BookDesignTemplates.com

Bible Engagement Basics/ Lawson W. Murray -- 1st ed.
ISBN 978-0-9951694-1-8

Soli Deo Gloria

Glory to God alone

He touches my tongue, His word to speak.

He guides my hands, His work to pursue.

He moves my feet, His way to tread.

He stirs my heart, His will to do.

ACKNOWLEDGEMENTS

The Bible is a corpus - a living tapestry of two stories - God's and ours - each connected to the other. Every thread illuminates our lives - each stitch reveals the Weaver who gives life. Broadly conceived, the tapestry portrays Jesus, and how we're woven in or out of His Story.

Writing a book is never a solo affair. I'm indebted to many people for their contributions:

Karen Murray. Thank you for praying, modelling Bible engagement in your daily life and journeying with me through the writing and publishing of this book.

Annabel Robinson is the editor of the online Bible reading guide, theStory™. Thank you for your guidance. You took this book up a notch as the content editor.

Julie Fitz-Gerald is a journalist and writer. Thank you for painstakingly reading and re-reading the content. Your word-smithing skills as the writing editor are appreciated.

Amy Csőke is the Director of Ministry Development at Scripture Union. Thank you for your creative flair and expertise with the cover design, formatting and typesetting.

Donald Tardif is the Directeur, Ligue pour la lecture de la Bible. Thank you for suggesting I write this book and for publishing Principes d'interaction avec la Bible.

Pierre Constant is Chair of New Testament Studies at Toronto Baptist Seminary and Chair of the Scripture Gift Mission Board. Thank you for reviewing the book's theology.

Christie Warren writes, performs and teaches Spoken Word. Thank you for your assistance on the chapter on Spoken Word. It would not have existed without you.

Thank you to colleagues at Scripture Union, Scripture Gift Mission and Ligue pour la lecture de la Bible. Your camaraderie, prayers and support are appreciated.

Thank you to colleagues at the Canadian Bible Forum and Forum of Bible Agencies North America. You helped me grow in my understanding of Bible engagement.

There's nothing new under the sun. I'm thankful for the writers from whom I've gleaned so much about Bible engagement. Their books are listed at the end of this book.

Most importantly, I thank Jesus for equipping me to write. The deficiencies in this book are wholly mine. Whatever is good and right and true is wholly from Him.

Beannachd Dia dhuit (Blessings of God be with you - Scottish Gaelic)
Anno Domini Nostri Iesu Christi 2017

RECOMMENDATIONS

This is such an important and timely book. From the opening pages, Bible Engagement Basics presents Scripture as God's Story: a Story we are a part of, and as we engage with it we discover we are not passive observers, we in fact are participants. The importance of engaging with this Story is outlined clearly, but to then present a huge variety of models and ideas for engaging with it places this book as a must-read for those of us with a passion for Scripture.

Adrian Blenkinsop, Youth Bible engagement specialist, Author of "The Bible According To Gen Z."

Bible Engagement Basics gives us a biblical, theological and practical foundation as to why Scripture is the key to our relationship with God, and then takes the all-important next step (often skipped) to give us a broad selection of engagement practices to help us all learn how to actually reflect on the Bible with depth. I highly recommend this book as the "go to" book about how to engage Scripture to engage God.

Phil Collins, Professor of Christian Educational Ministries, Taylor University, Executive Director (Training and Content) Taylor Center for Scripture Engagement.

Bible Engagement Basics is filled with wisdom. It is a rallying call to get God's words inside of us so that the Word might become flesh again and again, read and known by everyone we meet (2 Cor. 3:2). But Lawson Murray's book is not just a rallying cry; it is filled with insight as to how to make this happen. Read this book and be changed!

Stephen G. Dempster, Professor of Religious Studies, Crandall University.

Whether you are finding for the first time the riches found within the Bible, or you are a seasoned teacher of the Bible, Lawson's book offers guideposts to going deeper. These guideposts are practical, encouraging and grounded in the experience of one who loves God and His Word.

Mark Forshaw, Chair, Forum of Bible Agencies - North America.

I suspected this was going to be a great book when I read "Bible engagement flows out of an intimate reciprocating relationship with Jesus." Yes! Besides the Christocentric foundation, I deeply appreciate the practical suggestions on how to engage Scripture and discover the riches of God's Word. I can hardly think of another book that does this better.

Mark Galli, Editor in Chief of Christianity Today.

Bible Engagement Basics gives the gift of perspective. This book gives readers practical coaching on how to engage with God's Word that will be meaningful to those who are new to the Bible or have been studying it for years.

Bobby Gruenewald, Founder of YouVersion and Innovation Leader at LifeChurch.tv

I am delighted that you are bringing out Bible Engagement Basics to encourage more people to read the Bible – the most powerful book that has ever been written.

Nicky Gumbel, Holy Trinity Brompton Vicar and pioneer of Alpha.

Bible Engagement Basics is a wise, practical, and extremely accessible introduction to engaging the Bible for transformation. I've been reading the Bible for many years and was happy to find new, creative ideas for my own engagement with the Scriptures. This is, quite frankly, one of the best books I've read for embracing the Bible ever more deeply.

Chris Hall, President of Renovaré.

Bible Engagement Basics assembles a cloud of witnesses to the indispensable role that the Bible plays in helping us know Jesus Christ. The book returns time and time again to the core issue: Bible engagement is Christ engagement; one is not the other and they shouldn't happen independently. All told, Lawson Murray gives us practical help and cause for deep reflection as to how we engage with Christ though his Word.

Rick Hiemstra, Director, Research and Media Relations, The Evangelical Fellowship of Canada.

Lawson Murray's excellent book Bible Engagement Basics offers a very readable overview of how we can connect with God in His Word. In so doing he's done what John Stott's "Understanding the Bible" did for a past generation; he's expressed the heartbeat of the global Scripture Union movement in a fresh new way.

Whitney T. Kuniholm, President Emeritus, Scripture Union USA.

Whatever you know about Bible engagement, you're sure to discover another approach in Bible Engagement Basics. Dr. Murray explores many approaches to Bible engagement, like the basics of reading, teaching and preaching God's Word. But he also encourages readers to use their imagination to enhance the experience. The common denominator to all of his approaches? They set us up for meaningful encounters with Jesus Christ so our lives are transformed in Him.

Roy L. Peterson, President & CEO, American Bible Society.

There is nothing more critical to Christian growth than learning to engage with the Bible. I wholeheartedly recommend this book as a comprehensive approach to doing just that. May God use this book to point many to The Book.

Janet Pope, speaker, blogger and author.

Many people think of the Bible as a text to dig into and learn new things about faith and life. And while there is much to learn in the Bible, Dr. Lawson Murray shows us how to think differently ... how Bible engagement is not about us digging into the Bible and learning new thoughts, it is about the Living Word of God digging into our lives and transforming us.

Paul Richardson, Chair, Forum of Bible Agencies International.

In our LifeWay Research study, we found that Bible engagement had the highest correlation with every other area of spiritual growth. We've all seen it - engaging the Bible is essential to spiritual growth. Now, you can be encouraged through Bible Engagement Basics to help you engage well!

Ed Stetzer, Billy Graham Distinguished Chair, Wheaton College.

Today, people with no idea of the nature or culture of the early church can hold in their hands letters written by apostles and others who guided new Christians, then and now, to explore and understand the Gospel. Bible Engagement Basics is an important furtherance of this as it empowers people globally to know the Scriptures and the Word of which it speaks.

Brian C Stiller, Global Ambassador, World Evangelical Alliance.

This is a wonderful, practical handbook for Christians wanting to engage with the Bible in a renewed way. I appreciated especially the reminder that for transformation (which we all want) to happen, we need to encounter and interact with Scripture, which for most of us can be a challenge at different times in our lives. Thank you for this inspiration and this book.

Karen Stiller, Senior Editor, Faith Today.

In a culture that speaks in story and image, here is an invaluable resource for moving the minds and hearts of your people from the Bible as The Word in words to the Bible as The Word in story, from the greatest story never told, or half told, or partially told, to The Greatest Story EVER Told.

Leonard Sweet, best-selling author, professor (Tabor College, Portland Seminary, Drew University), and founder and chief contributor to preachthestory.com

Lawson has called this book 'basics' – but it will take you much further than that implies! He looks at questions of how we experience Scripture, how we meet Jesus in the story, and how the Bible is integral to our lives as disciples. Lawson doesn't ignore the difficulties in engaging with the Bible, but I think it's fair to say he doesn't dwell on them either – his heart is for encouraging us on. This is a book that inspires me to action and to practice, and reminds me that I will never reach the end of my experience of Scripture, or its impact in my life and the world.

Danielle Welch, Executive Director, Lifewords UK & International.

We call ourselves "People of the Book," but many find the slow meditative reading that lets it sink into our hearts hard to do. This book is filled with suggestions to help you find approaches to taking in the Scriptures. Pastors and leaders will find in it a rich and thoughtful biblical theology of Bible engagement.

James C. Wilhoit, Professor of Core Studies and Scripture Press Professor of Christian Education, Wheaton College.

CONTENTS

PRELUDE 3

SECTION ONE - PRINCIPLES 6

Bible 7

Engagement 12

Theology 16

Story 20

Transformation 24

Purpose 28

Theme 32

Authority 36

Truth 39

Discipline 42

SECTION TWO - PRACTICES 44

Listening 46

Reading 50

Personal reading 53

Communal Reading 58

Public Reading 62

Reading Methods 65

Synthesizing 72

Analyzing 76

Studying 79

Interpreting 85

Contemplating 94

Imaging 100

Reflecting 104

Praying.. 108

Memorizing.. 114

Journaling... 118

Spoken Word... 122

Singing.. 126

Preaching.. 131

Teaching... 137

Applying... 142

SECTION THREE - PARADIGMS............... 148

Children.. 150

Centennials... 158

Millennials.. 165

Adults.. 170

Seniors.. 175

Families... 179

Small Groups.. 182

Churches... 188

Pastors.. 193

POSTSCRIPT.. 199

PRAYER.. 204

RECOMMENDED RESOURCES............... 205

THE AUTHOR.. 213

PRELUDE

We should settle it in our minds that everything the Father and the Son say to us in and through Scripture relates, one way or another, to the person, place and purpose of Christ, to the realities of God's kingdom and to faithful following of Christ through what Bunyan called the wilderness of this world. That is what the Christian Bible is all about, and we are not to go off at tangents away from this when we read it.

J. I. Packer, "Truth and Power: The Place of Scripture in the Christian Life."

There's a problem. Nine out of 10 Christians do not hold a biblical worldview, i.e., know what the Bible says and live according to its principles. Less than 20 percent of people who own a Bible will read it from cover to cover, and many people who say they're Christian say they're too busy or have no time to read the Bible.

American theology professor Telford Work identifies the enormity of the problem when he says, "Lay people, pastors, theologians, even entire traditions are confused about what the Bible is, and what roles it plays in the life of their communities. They scratch their heads more than ever, wondering how they should be reading their Bibles."

Yes, there's a problem, but this book isn't about the problem. This book's about solutions - about what the Bible is, why we should engage it, and what role it should play in our private and communal lives.

This book introduces us to the principles, practices and paradigms that can help us strengthen our connections with God's Story. One of my friends says, "It's an amazing collection of resources and an encyclopedia of practical suggestions for getting into the Bible." As such, each chapter invites fresh encounters with God's Story, champions Bible engagement, or equips individuals and communities with biblical strategies, approaches, tools or resources that work.

The vision for this book is not to help more people read the Bible (though that will hopefully be a by-product). The low ebb in Bible reading isn't really the problem. The real problem is relational - people aren't connected with Jesus. It's an age old problem. Two thousand years ago people had the Word. What they needed was the One who made the Word flesh!

The Bible is a God-given window through which we get the best view of Jesus. It's therefore crucial that we connect with the Bible to connect with Him. That's what this book is about - connecting us with God's Story in ways that lead to meaningful encounters with Jesus Christ and our lives being progressively transformed in Him.

So who is this book for? It's for Christians who need to discover Bible engagement is the way of life for God's people, not an extracurricular activity. It's for Christian leaders, pastors, teachers, congregations, and believers who identify that Bible reading alone is not enough. And it's for anyone who wants to know the "how to" of practically improving and enhancing their engagement with the Bible.

Concerning the structure of the book: For ease of reference, the book is divided into three sections: Principles, Practices and Paradigms. The chapters in each section are intentionally short and pithy, aiming to give you the essence of the Bible engagement topic so that you know enough to act on it. Each chapter, while being part of the whole book, can also stand alone.

Ultimately, this book is about the benefits of Bible engagement. It will help you discover why Bible engagement is the best thing you can do for yourself, your family, your church and your community. Am I exaggerating? Read this book, put it into practice, and let me know what happens. I'm confident you'll see change in all these areas!

PRINCIPLES

While most books provide the reader with a preface or dust cover that indicates what the stories are about, there is one book that stands alone: the Bible.

The Bible is unlike other books. It doesn't have a prelude explaining its theme and it doesn't indicate why the writers wrote it. While modern day Bibles sometimes include blurbs from the publishers, they don't give details about how it's substantively different to every other book. Yet it's a book where we can find our part amongst its pages. And it's a book that reaches beyond its pages with the power to completely transform our lives.

When I started reading the Bible I didn't know what made it different to other books, why it was holy and why it supposedly had a claim on my life. In fact it took me many years before I clearly identified the purpose of the Bible, understood its unique authority, and discovered the primary theme.

As you begin this book my intention is to help you fast-track what took me decades to learn. Section 1 establishes the core foundational principles that inform and undergird Bible engagement. When you read this section you'll discover what the Bible says about itself, the beliefs that support Bible engagement, the purpose of the Bible, and some key reasons why we should connect with the Bible. When you finish this section you'll have a basic understanding of the propositions on which the practices and paradigms of Bible engagement are built.

BIBLE

We love God's Word in the Scriptures of the Old and New Testament, echoing the joyful delight of the Psalmist in the Torah, "I love your commands more than gold ... Oh how I love your law." We receive the whole Bible as the Word of God, inspired by God's Spirit, spoken and written through human authors. We submit to it as supremely and uniquely authoritative, governing our belief and our behaviour. We testify to the power of God's Word to accomplish His purpose of salvation. We affirm that the Bible is the final written word of God, not surpassed by any further revelation, but we also rejoice that the Holy Spirit illumines the minds of God's people so that the Bible continues to speak God's truth in fresh ways to people in every culture.

The Lausanne Movement.

The right way to begin a book on Bible engagement is with the Bible itself as it reminds us that, *"Blessed is the one who does not walk in step with the wicked or stand in the way that sinners take or sit in the company of mockers, but whose delight is in the law of the Lord, and who meditates on his law day and night. That person is like a tree planted by streams of water,*

*which yields its fruit in season and whose leaf does not wither -
whatever they do prospers"* Psalm 1:1-3.

As foundational truth for everything that follows, here are
20 texts from the Bible about the Bible:

It's God-breathed. *"All Scripture is God-breathed and is useful
for teaching, rebuking, correcting and training in righteousness"*
2 Timothy 3:16.

It's eternal. *"All your words are true; all your righteous laws
are eternal"* Psalm 119:160.

It stands firm. *"Your word, Lord, is eternal; it stands firm in
the heavens"* Psalm 119:89.

It's flawless. *"Every word of God is flawless"* Proverbs 30:5.

It's truth. *"Your word is truth"* John 17:17.

It's alive. *"For the word of God is alive and active. Sharper than
any double-edged sword, it penetrates even to dividing soul and
spirit, joints and marrow; it judges the thoughts and attitudes
of the heart"* Hebrews 4:12.

It's a light. *"Your word is a lamp for my feet, a light on my
path"* Psalm 119:105.

It's like fire. *"'Is not my word like fire,' declares the Lord, 'and
like a hammer that breaks a rock in pieces?'"* Jeremiah 23:29.

It's more precious than gold. *"The decrees of the Lord are firm, and all of them are righteous. They are more precious than gold, than much pure gold; they are sweeter than honey, than honey from the honeycomb"* Psalm 19:9-10.

It's wonderful. *"Your statutes are wonderful"* Psalm 119:129.

It gives understanding. *"The unfolding of your words gives light; it gives understanding to the simple"* Psalm 119:130.

It gives joy. *"The precepts of the Lord are right, giving joy to the heart"* Psalm 19:8.

It combats sin. *"I have hidden your word in my heart that I might not sin against you"* Psalm 119:11.

It's refreshing. *"The law of the Lord is perfect, refreshing the soul"* Psalm 19:7.

It's for your hearts and minds. *"Fix these words of mine in your hearts and minds; tie them as symbols on your hands and bind them on your foreheads"* Deuteronomy 11:18.

It should be on your lips. *"Keep this Book of the Law always on your lips; meditate on it day and night, so that you may be careful to do everything written in it. Then you will be prosperous and successful"* Joshua 1:8.

It should be obeyed. *"Do not merely listen to the word, and so deceive yourselves. Do what it says"* James 1:22.

It leads to blessing. *"But whoever looks intently into the perfect law that gives freedom, and continues in it - not forgetting what they have heard, but doing it - they will be blessed in what they do"* James 1:25.

It should have nothing added or subtracted from it. *"See that you do all I command you; do not add to it or take away from it"* Deuteronomy 12:32.

It endures forever. *"The grass withers and the flowers fall, but the word of our God endures forever"* Isaiah 40:8.

It will never pass away. *"Heaven and earth will pass away, but my words will never pass away"* Matthew 24:35.

ENGAGEMENT

Bible engagement is peeling back the covers of God's Word to discover the hopes and promises of the Bible and discovering what God has to say to you, no matter what your situation; that results in hearts changed, lives transformed and an unrelenting drive to be like Jesus to this broken world.

Forum of Bible Agencies - North America.

Connecting with God's Word is foundational and imperative for God's people. *"Get them (the Scriptures) inside of you and then get them inside your children"* Deuteronomy 6:7 (MSG).

So how do we get the Scriptures inside of us and inside of our children, i.e., how do we engage with the Bible? While this question will be answered in multiple ways throughout the chapters that follow, this chapter will help us understand what we mean by the term "Bible engagement."

Bible engagement is the process that connects us with the Bible so that we have meaningful encounters with Jesus Christ in order for our lives to be progressively transformed in Him.

To elaborate: Bible engagement happens through the course of our lives as we find our part in God's Story. For Bible engagement to happen we must first come together with and develop a vital relationship with Christ. The relationship begins and proceeds by grace and through faith as Christ saves us from sin and sanctifies us by the Spirit. Bible engagement is evidenced through ongoing obedience to God's Word that's seen in life-changes that take place individually and in community.

> The motivation for reading, reflecting, remembering and responding to the Word is only as strong as our love for Christ.

Four primary Bible engagement actions

According to James 1:17-25 there are four actions involved in Bible engagement:

1. Receive God's Word - "humbly accept" James 1:21.
2. Reflect on God's Word - "looks intently" James 1:25.
3. Remember God's Word - "not forgetting" James 1:25.
4. Respond to God's Word - "doing it" James 1:22-23, 25.

Bible engagement essentials

To effectively receive, reflect, remember and respond to God's Word there are several things we need to know:

1. Bible engagement flows out of an intimate reciprocating relationship with Jesus. The motivation for reading, reflecting, remembering and responding to the Word is only as strong as our love for Christ. The more we love Jesus, the greater our drive to engage with His Word will be.

2. Bible engagement is a process. There are no shortcuts. It involves what the scholar and author Eugene Peterson calls "a long obedience in the same direction" - a course of action that's repeated over and over again through the ups and downs of life.

3. Bible engagement involves desire. When our desire to read, reflect, remember and respond to the Word is greater than staying where we are, we'll be on the way toward regular and consistent engagement with the Word.

4. Bible engagement requires discipline. Daily choices about how we prioritize our time must be made in order to grow stronger in our engagement with God's Word. Praying or hoping for a better connection with the Bible is futile if we spend our time glued to the TV or consumed by social media.

5. Bible engagement is fuelled by the Holy Spirit. "The same Holy Spirit who inspired Bible authors to write, inspires Bible readers to understand and accept it, as God's Word," says David Jackman, president of the Proclamation Trust. Self-efforts to improve our engagement with the Bible will end in failure. We'll only mature in reading, reflection, remembering and responding to the Word when we seek the daily filling of the Spirit (Ephesians 5:18). Real Bible engagement is initiated and enabled when we recognize our impotence - then invite the Holy Spirit to equip us as we listen, learn and live out God's Word.

6. Bible engagement is a challenge. The enemy of God, Satan, does not want us to engage with the Bible. The spiritual forces of darkness work actively to distract, divert, daunt, deceive or defeat us when we seek to read, reflect, remember and respond to God's Word.

7. Bible engagement results in action. In the Parable of the Sower the climax of the story comes when people *"hear the word, accept it, and produce a crop"* Mark 4:20. When reading and hearing the Bible results in people becoming living epistles, i.e., being life words, then Bible engagement has occurred. Producing a crop is the ultimate goal. It's not enough to hear the Word and accept it; the inward must become outward - the concealed must be revealed.

THEOLOGY

Scripture engagement is interaction with the biblical text in a way that provides sufficient opportunity for the text to speak for itself by the power of the Holy Spirit, enabling readers and listeners to hear the voice of God and discover for themselves the unique claim Jesus Christ is making upon them.

Fergus Macdonald, Taylor University Center for Scripture Engagement.

There are 10 theological assumptions that frame Bible engagement. A holistic theology includes the following:

1. Bible engagement incorporates three basic elements. The three elements are: connecting with God's Word, facilitating an encounter with Christ, and pursuing progressive transformation. The elements are interconnected and substantive. When we engage with the Bible the three elements should function together.

2. Bible engagement should have a strong Christological focus. Scripture invites us to connect with the person, attributes and life of Christ. We should know the Word of God and know the God of the Word. It's much more than connecting people with a book to be read or listened to. It's about connecting with the One of whom the Bible speaks – Jesus Christ.

3. Bible engagement should be relational. We must personally meet with and grow in association with Christ both interpersonally (with a living person) and intrapersonally (with a Spirit person). It's about learning to love and be loved, about knowing and being known, about friendship and being a friend, about living and letting live. In order to personally meet with and grow in association with Christ, we must believe that He was born, lived, died and was raised from the dead, and accept that this happened in order to reconcile us with God. The relationship that's formed with Christ is experiential, intimate and interactive, much like an earthly marriage.

> Bible engagement must be more than connecting with a book. It should be a connection with the Story.

4. Bible engagement is not a one-off or arbitrary action. It's a journey - something that should proceed forward step by step. It takes time and happens cumulatively over the course of days, months and many years. Well known Evangelical leader and English cleric John Stott once said, "Only as we continue to appropriate by faith the riches of Christ ... disclosed to us in Scripture shall we grow into spiritual maturity, and become men and women of God ... thoroughly equipped for every good work."

5. Bible engagement is a two-way street. When we connect with the Bible we must do so in a way that allows the Bible to have its way with us. Bible engagement is not strictly an individual affair. The Bible must have its way with us personally and communally.

6. Bible engagement should be thought of as a verb. It involves exertion and energy, imitating Christ, and putting what we learn from Him into practice. According to Stott, "Scripture bears witness to Christ not in order to satisfy our curiosity, but in order to draw from us a response of faith."

7. Bible engagement must be more than connecting with a book. It should be a connection with the Story of the triune God so that a person's or a community's story intersects with, is changed by, and finds its place in the Story. "Christians have not merely inherited a founding document containing a narrative; they themselves are also actually part of that narrative, or story," explain the British theologians, Colin Greene and Martin Robinson.

8. Bible engagement is connecting with a unified story or narrative. First and foremost the Bible is God's Story. To understand it one needs to know the basic rules of narratology. When we engage the Bible as narrative we will learn how to indwell the story and open ourselves to be changed by its wisdom.

9. Bible engagement is simultaneously a discontinuity with the world and the way to effectively renew the world. For Bible engagement to be effective we must pursue a counter-cultural life style (1 John 2:15-17) while at the same time seeking to be salt and light to the world (Matthew 5:13-16).

10. Bible engagement is beneficial. When we read, reflect, remember and respond to God's Word we will be sure of our salvation (1 John 5:13), grow spiritually (1 Peter 2:2), have victory over temptation (Ephesians 6:13-17), be infused with power (Hebrews 4:12), be strong (1 John 2:14), pray with confidence (John 15:7), have joy (John 15:11), know peace (John 16:33), and be blessed (Luke 11:28).

STORY

Humanity is telling its own story, improvising scenarios, creating roles for itself - for all the other creatures, too, and of course for God! The roles that humanity creates are - in the view of these witnesses to God's story - almost always not the roles intended for it. Humanity does not have any real aptitude for the parts that it writes for itself. Yet it seems to be perfectly at liberty to experiment very widely.

Douglas John Hall, "Thinking the Faith."

Story is the narrative, saga, and drama of the Bible. It's more than an arrangement of facts, ideas, propositions, or a compilation of spiritual laws. Story describes an account that is unified, immediate, multidimensional, relational, non-manipulative, unique and central to knowing truth and the One who is Truth. It is a spacious realm that we are invited to enter into with imagination and faith, and once we have entered, to see ourselves as participants. Story invites us to actively engage and get caught up in God's saga by receiving it and reenacting it.

Story is integral to Bible engagement because it brings shape and structure to the Bible. The popular writer and theologian

Scot McKnight says, "The unity of the Bible is this Story. It is the Story that puts the Bible together. Our grand systems do not form the unity of the Bible; the Story that God tells, forms and frames that unity."

God's Story is the supreme Story. It's the true story about life that promises and delivers abundant life. It demands a hearing! When we engage with the Story, it makes sense of all the other stories of our lives. "When it is internalized and it becomes your story, it gives meaning in the midst of meaninglessness and value in the midst of worthlessness," say veteran college professors Preben Vang and Terry Carter.

The story for Christians begins when our personal stories unite with and are reconfigured in the light of God's Story. Explicitly, the story for Christians is formed by God's Story when we indwell the whole Story; when we're grounded in creation, discover the disconnect in the Fall, find redemption and reconciliation through Christ's death and resurrection, and become actively part of the church.

> Bible engagement only moves forward when we respond to the Great Storyteller (God) as He invites us to step into the roles intended for us.

The meeting of our stories with God's Story is not a simple affair. Encounters between people and God are complicated and convoluted. This is due, not to God, but to us. We have a tendency to confuse, digress and destroy. The problem is that we're inclined to create an alternative story to the story God invites us to participate in. In our ignorance, makeshift settings are created, distorted roles are developed, and conflicting dramas are enacted.

When we enter into the Story in the way God intends, an elemental reconfiguration occurs that "creates a new world, a new history, a new possibility of fresh adventures, a new imagined opportunity, most certainly not just one damn thing after the other, and most certainly not just the duties and responsibilities that history allows us to discharge," say Greene and Robinson. That's because the Story is primary and history is merely the by-product of how we do or do not live our lives according to the Story.

Because the Story has a life of its own, Bible engagement only moves forward when we respond to the Great Storyteller (God) as He invites us to step into the roles intended for us. The roles are many and varied, including listening, speaking, reading, studying, reciting, memorizing, interpreting, singing, preaching, receiving, or acting – both individually and communally.

All our spiritual senses need to be engaged with the Story. We need to *"taste and see that the Lord is good"* (Psalm 34:8); open our eyes to the Story (Psalm 119:18, 82); and open our ears to the Story – *"He who has ears to hear, let him hear"* Mark 4:9. As we engage our spiritual senses with the Story there's a growing realization that the Bible isn't about God in our stories, but rather our stories in God's Story.

In order for our stories to be immersed in God's Story we must read the Bible as the story of our past, present and future. To indwell the Story we must remember what was, embrace what is, and picture what's to come. This happens when we reflect on what God said, live out what God directs us to do, and get ready for what God's prepared for us (cf. John 14:1-4).

If the Bible is reduced to a handbook for church dogma, a moral rule book, or a collection of wise sayings to guide us through life, it's easy for us to take it or leave it. But when the Bible is shared, in the power of the Spirit, as the Story which runs deeper than the world's stories, it invites us to enter into a different world and see ourselves in a different light, that is - to share God's view of the world.

TRANSFORMATION

Transformation occurs when scripture is viewed as a place of encounter with God that is approached by yielding the false self and its agenda, by opening one's self unconditionally to God, and by a hunger to respond in love to whatever God desires.

Robert Mulholland, "Shaped by the Word: The Power of Scripture in Spiritual Formation."

Transformation, the process of change whereby a person becomes progressively more Christ-like (Galatians 6:15), goes hand in hand with Bible engagement. There are three aspects to transformation:

Salvation. Transformation does not happen naturally and does not come easily. The prophet asks, *"Can the Ethiopian change his skin or the leopard his spots?"* Jeremiah 13:23. There's no outside force that can change us to become more like Christ. Something internal is required. Transformation begins when we realize that *"the whole head is sick and the whole heart faint"* (Isaiah 1:5) and it continues when forgiveness for sin is sought and received (Psalm 13:5) through faith in Christ as *"the propitiation for our sins"* 1 John 2:2.

The good news in God's Word is that our hearts can be changed. God reveals and communicates His love for us so that we hear and believe. When the human heart (our integrated value systems, beliefs, experiences, motivations, and the reality of who we are) responds to God's love, it transcends who we are. *"For it is with your heart that you believe and are justified"* Romans 10:10.

Bible engagement is about connecting our hearts with God's heart. "Our very reading and interpretation of Scripture is shaped by the hearts we bring to the text," say professors James Wilhoit and Evan Howard. Transformation therefore occurs when our engagement with the Word of God becomes an encounter with Christ. The Apostle Paul alludes to this when he says, *"I pray also that the eyes of your heart may be enlightened in order that you may know the hope to which he has called you, the riches of his glorious inheritance in the saints, and his incomparably great power for us who believe"* Ephesians 1:18-19.

Sanctification. It's in our hearts that we unite with God at the deepest level and grow into Christ-likeness. When the heart is cleansed from sin by the word of truth (John 17:17) a right relationship with Christ is formed (Romans 10:10), Christ's nature lives in us through the Holy Spirit (1 Corinthians 3:16), and love for Christ ensues (Mark 12:30).

God's Word transforms lives. It's in and through the transference of God's Word that our hearts are touched and reprogrammed (Ezekiel 36:26). When, in the power of the Spirit, we interact with the Word, both personally and communally, God speaks into our hearts in ways that nurture us to live only all for Him. In contrast, when we ignore God's Word, we impair our spiritual development.

God uses His Word to mature us. In order for God's Word to transform our hearts, Bible engagement requires new postures of authenticity, vulnerability and consecration. It's only when we open our hearts fully and prayerfully, that God will fully apply His Word - thereby making us new creations with the capacity to worship Him and do good works.

Sanctification requires transformed thinking (Romans 12:1-2). "As God renews our minds with Scripture, we begin to think biblically so that we can live biblically," says teacher and author Janet Pope. To think biblically we must know God's Word. If we don't know God's Word, we won't know what He wants us to do. If we don't know what He wants us to do, we open ourselves to the influence of false teachers, our own desires, Satan, and the deceptive philosophies based on the principles of the world (Colossians 2:8).

> In order for God's Word to transform our hearts, Bible engagement requires new postures of authenticity, vulnerability and consecration.

Service. The Bible makes claims on our lives. When God's Word courses through us, we're transformed for a purpose. *"For we are God's workmanship, created in Christ Jesus to do good works, which God prepared in advance for us to do"* Ephesians 2:10.

Bible engagement is more than words; it's actions. It's whole-heartedly worshipping, witnessing and working for Christ. "God's plan for believers involves total dedication to knowing and following His Word," insists Pope. It's all or nothing. Transformation is seen to be at work in our lives when we obey the Word and live it out every day. It's not enough to say we love Christ; we must act on the truth (1 John 3:18). *"But if anyone obeys his word, love for God is truly made complete in them"* 1 John 2:5.

PURPOSE

What I began to see was that the Bible is not essentially, as I had always more or less supposed, a book of ethical principles, of moral exhortations, of cautionary tales about exemplary people, of uplifting thoughts - in fact, not really a religious book at all in the sense that most of the books you would be apt to find in a minister's study or reviewed in a special religion issue of the New York Times book section are religious. I saw it instead as a great, tattered compendium of writings, the underlying and unifying purpose of all of which is to show how God works through the Jacobs and Jabboks of history to make himself known to the world and to draw the world back to himself.

Frederick Buechner, "Now and Then."

Why should we read and hear the Bible? Is it for moralistic reasons - reading and hearing the Bible as an example to imitate? Is it for intellectual stimulus - reading and hearing the Bible as something to know? Is it for therapeutic grounds - reading and hearing the Bible to feel better about ourselves? Is it for theological acumen - reading and hearing the Bible to systematically develop religious beliefs? Is it for guidance - reading and hearing the Bible to get direction for our lives?

While many people read and hear the Bible for these and many other reasons, the fundamental purpose of Bible reading and hearing is to let the Bible have its way with us.

The Bible is the Book of books because it's one of a kind - without equal. It's without equal because it's alive (Hebrews 4:12). Because it's alive, the Bible wants to have its way with us. Bible reader and hearer beware! The Bible "will have a man's or woman's heart and soul, and if not, it will work despair ... whoever you are, if you do not repent and believe the testimony laid down in this book concerning God and his Christ, it will ... render your reading of it, your interpretation of it, your preaching on it a comic spectacle to the world to which you believed you had to adjust it," warns Lutheran theologian Roy Harrisville.

The single word encapsulating what it means for the Bible to have its way with us is "transformation." In order for transformation to occur, "encounter" and "interaction" are required. Encounter and interaction are best facilitated through relationship. If the Bible is going to have its way with us, we must have a relationship with the Author. To have a relationship with the Author, we must connect with and live in obedience to the One of whom the Bible speaks - Jesus Christ.

If the purpose of Bible reading and hearing is to let the Bible have its way with us, i.e., transform us through encounter and interaction with Jesus Christ, then Bible reading and hearing is about interaction with the Word in ways that reveal God, expose sin, and cause us to worship Him. For this to happen, we need "Jesus engagement."

So what is Jesus engagement? It's connecting with the One who is the Word so that His Spirit can reveal, renew and revive us, in and through the Word, to love and live for Him in accordance with His Word. In short, it's a dynamic life-changing connection with the risen, reigning Jesus Himself.

If we love the Word more than we love the One who is the Word, we've missed the mark. Bible reading and hearing, in and of itself, doesn't necessarily lead to us loving and living for Jesus.

God's given us His Word to lead us to Christ - to know Jesus and make Him known. We can be "Bible-believing," but if we're not "Christ-centred" we're not letting the Bible control us. It's only when we embrace Christ as the unity and unfolding message of the whole of Scripture that the Bible gets to have its way with us.

The Pharisees and teachers of the law are an example of ardent Bible readers and hearers who got it wrong. Their hearts were captivated by the Word, but not taken captive by the God of the Word. This resulted in legalism and a love for their own traditions. Jesus called them out for this, saying: *"These people honour me with their lips, but their hearts are far from me"* (Mark 7:6) and *"thus you nullify the word of God by your tradition"* Mark 7:13. That is, their Bible reading or hearing perpetuated religious rituals and stifled spiritual life, nothing more.

> The primary purpose of Bible reading and hearing is to engage with Jesus - to discover how our stories should embrace and live out His Story.

That's not to say that reading and hearing the Bible isn't a required spiritual discipline; it most definitely is. But it is to say that our reasons for reading and hearing the Bible have to centre on a vital, ongoing, life-altering relationship with Christ. As Stott reminds us, "Only as we continue to appropriate by faith the riches of Christ which are disclosed to us in Scripture shall we grow into spiritual maturity, and become men and women of God who are thoroughly equipped for every good work."

Let's be clear about why we read and hear the Bible. If Bible reading and hearing is emphasized simply for the sake of Bible reading and hearing, it falls short of God's intent for His Word. The primary purpose of Bible reading and hearing is to engage with Jesus - to discover how our stories should embrace and live out His Story. So let's "get beyond propositions and Bible verses to Christ. I do not mean 'get around' Bible verses, but 'through' Bible verses to Christ, to the person, the living person, to know Him, cherish Him, treasure Him, enjoy Him, trust Him, be at home with Him," explains preacher and author John Piper.

THEME

The entire Scriptures, both Old and New Testaments, are unified by a common narrative. And once our eyes are opened to see that narrative, everything in both Testaments gels into a coherent, understandable, and amazing story. And what is that story? It's the story of Jesus Christ.

Frank Viola & Leonard Sweet, "Jesus: A Theography."

The theme of the Bible is not a principle, concept, set of values, ethics to be learned, spiritual sayings, collection of doctrines, snapshots of God, or a storehouse of propositions. The theme of the Bible is a person to be known. While there are many sub-themes in the Bible - like justice, peace, redemption, salvation or restoration - there's a grand theme that begins in Genesis and weaves its way through the 66 books. The theme of the Bible, about which everything else revolves, is the One who was, who is, and who is to come. From beginning to end, the theme of the Bible is Jesus Christ.

Some people say they don't understand the Bible. They may not understand it because the theme of the Bible may be a mystery to them. Only when the theme is known, do the contents become clear. As theologian and apologist Norman

Geisler notes, "To understand the Bible, look for Jesus." To understand the Bible we must know that, "In every part of both Testaments, Christ is to be found - dimly and indistinctly at the beginning - more clearly and plainly in the middle - fully and completely at the end - but really and substantially everywhere," said the 19th century Anglican clergyman J. C. Ryle.

Christ Himself taught that He is the central theme of the Bible. He is the message and mediator of its meaning, the link between the Testaments, the content of the canon, and the unity of every book.

> From beginning to end, the theme of the Bible is Jesus Christ.

This is plainly revealed in the Gospel. Walking to Emmaus with two disciples, He began with Moses and the Prophets to explain to them what was said in all the Scriptures concerning Himself (Luke 24:27).

When the religious leaders didn't identify Christ as the main reason for God's revelation, He confronted them saying, *"You study the Scriptures diligently because you think that in them you have eternal life. These are the very Scriptures that testify about me, yet you refuse to come to me to have life."* John 5:39-40. There was no wiggle-room for the religious leaders and there's no wiggle-room for us; the Scriptures are all about Christ - and if we fail to see that, we miss the forest for the trees.

Martin Luther, the champion of sola scriptura (Scripture alone) and solo Christo (Christ alone), said, "In the whole Scripture, there is nothing but Christ, either in plain words or involved words ... The whole Scripture is about Christ alone everywhere, if we look to its inner meaning, though superficially it may sound different ... It is beyond question that all Scriptures point to Christ alone." Simply stated, Stott affirms, "Jesus is the focus of Scripture." Similarly, teacher and pastor Edmund Clowney says, "The Bible is the greatest storybook, not just because it is full of wonderful stories but because it tells one great story, the story of Jesus."

To reduce the theme of the Bible to anything less than Christ is to miss the point of the Bible. Christ is more than a starting point for reading, reflecting, remembering, and responding to God's Word; He's the central point for the way we interpret and apply the Scriptures (John 1:18). This is true for both the Old Testament where Christ is veiled and the New Testament where Christ is clearly seen.

All the sub-themes of the Bible flow from Christ and fit together because of Him. Every literary form in the Bible (narrative, prophecy, poetry, teaching, etc.) unfolds a story that's ultimately about Christ. Christ brings unity and coherence to Bible engagement. He's the life-blood, the very pulse of the Bible. He's the lens that brings Scripture into focus, the key that unlocks truth, the thread that secures, and the One who knits together the unity of the storyline from promise to fulfillment.

If Jesus made Himself the central theme of the Bible, then to know the Bible we must know Him. Knowing Christ is the prerequisite to effective Bible engagement. To know Him, we must align our hearts, minds, and wills with Him. The aligning of our hearts, minds and wills with Christ begins with confession of sin, contrition, repentance, and faith in Christ alone to save and sanctify us.

Not knowing Christ results in a Bible engagement malfunction. If we do not immerse ourselves in Christ by becoming what McKnight calls "a People of the Story" we cannot engage with the Bible. In fact, any misrepresentation or misunderstanding about Christ ends in a contortion or collapse in our understanding of the Bible; which in turn ends in an inability to see God as He really is.

Dutch theologian G. C. Berkouwer asserted, "Every word about the God-breathed character of Scripture is meaningless if Holy Scripture is not understood as the witness concerning Christ." And the second Vatican Council add, "For ignorance of the Scriptures is ignorance of Christ." So when we engage with the Scriptures, let's do so with Christ as the centre, inner reason, joyful hope, intimate friend, and compelling end.

AUTHORITY

It is enormously important that we see the role of scripture not simply as being to provide true information about, or even an accurate running commentary upon, the work of God in salvation and new creation, but as taking an active part within that ongoing purpose.

N. T. Wright, "Scripture and the Authority of God."

Bible engagement rests on the belief that there should be an unswerving acknowledgement and commitment to the centrality and authority of the Bible.

The Bible is authoritative because all authority belongs to God and is of God. In the Old Testament, the Father exercises authority through the creation of all that is, through His dealings with His people, and through many significant events. In the New Testament, Christ exercises and claims all authority (Matthew 28:18).

The Bible is also authoritative because God speaks and sustains His Word. Bible engagement rests on the understanding that the Spirit gives life to the Word and does so by enabling the reader or listener to hear the Word and live it out.

A point of order is necessary at this juncture. A central insight of the Reformation is that God is the absolute authority. If God is the absolute authority then the Bible can't contend for that authority. How then, if the authority of the Bible cannot be considered absolute, should its authority be understood? The answer to this question, according to the Anglican scholar N. T. Wright, is that the authority of Scripture is "delegated or mediated ... from that which God himself possesses." So when we use the phrase "the authority of the Bible," it can only make sense if it's a shorthand for "the authority of ... God exercised ... through Scripture."

> Bible engagement can't happen if we do not surrender our inclination to control God.

To continue, the purpose or goal of authority is to bring us to a place of liberty - to set us free so that we come to know fullness of life in Christ Jesus (John 10:10). God expresses His authority through judging and condemning sin in the world in a way which will save and sanctify people. His intent is to redeem and remake the world, through the sovereign exercise of His power and love, so that we can be fully human.

Scripture texts like Romans 15:4, 2 Timothy 3:16-17, and Hebrews 4:12 indicate that the Bible is an integral component in God's plan, i.e., it's part of the means by which God directs the process of salvation and sanctification. Wright says that the Bible "is designed to function through human beings, through the church, through people who, living still by the Spirit, have their life molded by this Spirit inspired book."

In recognizing that the Bible is designed to function through us, then the exercise of God's authority to make us fully human is not an end in itself. God saves and sanctifies us for a purpose. Our purpose is to do what Jesus did (John 20:21). We are to go into the world to speak and enact His will. The Great Commandment (Matthew 22:37-39) and the Great Commission (Matthew 28:19-20), in particular, serve to direct us to these ends.

All told, Bible engagement can only happen when we submit our authority to God's authority. It's hypocrisy to affirm the authority of the Scriptures but functionally disobey them in our everyday lives. We cannot and must not usurp God's authority by replacing it with self-sovereignty. Bible engagement can't happen if we do not surrender our inclination to control God. Quite simply, when we engage with the Word we cannot and should not try to fit God into our preconceived ideas of what He should be like or what He should do.

The Bible is not an end in itself. God is God - we must receive His Word as people under His authority and act on it in ways that bring honour and glory to Him. That's not to say that coming under the authority of God and His Word is a fait accompli for most of us. Oxford academic director Ida Glaser observes that, "In fact, none of us starts by accepting God's revelation in Christ or in the Bible ... we need God to lead us to this understanding and he leads us all in different ways."

TRUTH

It's fantastic to realize - and sometimes I think we forget it - that every time we pick up the Bible, we pick up the truth. What a tremendous legacy we have. But we can't take it for granted, and we certainly can't let it just sit around. So the first reason I believe we need to study the Word of God is that it's the source of truth.

John MacArthur, "How To Study The Bible."

Can we conclude from what's been said about the authority of the Bible that the Bible is truthful? At first blush this appears to be a scandalous question. After all, if the Bible is authoritative because all authority abides in God, and God is described in the Bible as the God of truth (2 Chronicles 15:3; Psalm 31:5), the One who speaks the truth (Isaiah 45:19) and the One who never lies (1 Samuel 15:29; Titus 1:2), then surely it is more than enough to say that the Bible is truthful.

In the current culture of relativism, when truth is what people make of it, the truthfulness of the Bible is often disputed. Disputes about the veracity of the Bible should be expected. They're also problematic. If we dismiss the truthfulness of the Bible we get caught in a hurricane of subjectivism, with everyone acting like a god, and everyone saying what should or should not be believed.

The root cause, however, of why people question the veracity of the Scriptures is because they don't know Christ. To know truth, we must first know the One through whom truth comes (John 1:17), is full of truth (John 1:14), who is the truth (John 14:6), and bears witness to the truth (John 18:37). Bible engagement requires submission to the Lordship of Christ. To engage with the Bible we must hold Christ's view of the Word. And Christ's view of the Word is that it's real, lasting, alive, about Him, is truth, and doesn't lie (Matthew 5:17-18, Luke 24:25-27, John 10:35, 17:17).

Foundational to reading and hearing God's Word is knowing that God and His Word are inseparable. When the Bible speaks, God speaks. Here's the point: The Bible is totally truthful and reliable, because the Bible originated with God. God's Word is truth because God's Word is bound to God Himself.

When we say that the Bible originated with God, we must add that God speaks through human writers with human language. God's Word is geographically, historically, culturally, socially and circumstantially linked to this world.

The writers each wrote in their own way, and their writings reflect their own distinct literary styles, personalities, and experiences. They wrote in the context of their time. But as they did so, *"they were carried along by the Holy Spirit"* (2 Peter 1:21) and God spoke through them *"at many times in various ways"* Hebrews 1:1.

The Bible is therefore both the word of God and the word of man. To say that the Bible is truthful is to say that God spoke truth through human writers and kept them from error without circumventing their humanity. It's also to say that men spoke truth, freely using their own words, yet without warping God's message.

So what does this say about the Bible's own veracity? In Psalm 19:7 it says that the law of the Lord is *temimah,* an adjective meaning faultless, whole or complete. In 2 Timothy 3:16 the word *theopneustos* is used, which means inspired or coming directly from God; literally *"is God-breathed."* And in 1 Peter 1:25 the phrase, *"the word of the Lord endures forever,"* indicates that God's Word is incapable of failing and permanently binding.

> God's Word is truth because God's Word is bound to God Himself.

Taken together; the Bible's claims of being whole, inspired and binding are like three legs of a stool. All three complement each other and all three are needed. If one or more of the legs are missing we can't read, reflect, remember or respond to the Bible as we should. Taken together and properly understood they help us see that what is God-breathed and sustained - the Word of God, in its context and as a whole - is complete, accurate, trustworthy, sufficient, right and true.

DISCIPLINE

The daily practice of Bible reading and reflection is essential for our spiritual health and growth. Yet most people don't read the Bible regularly.

One of the reasons why so few people read and reflect on God's Word may be because we lack discipline. We lack discipline when we don't assert our willpower over our more basic desires, i.e., when we don't do what we know is best.

The dictionary defines a disciplined person as someone who's established a goal and is willing to achieve that goal at the expense of his or her individuality. Bible engagement requires work and discipline. A healthy faith doesn't happen automatically. Spiritual health and growth require a lifetime commitment. The number one thing we must do to grow spiritually is meet with God in and through His Word every day. There are no shortcuts. We must show up regularly to read, reflect, remember and respond to God's Word.

If you're thinking, "That's easier said than done," you're right. Bible engagement undertaken as a solo affair usually fails. If we rely, as we often do, on our own strength and willpower, we'll come up short.

So if we can't muster enough mental discipline to faithfully and consistently engage with God's Word, are we doomed to fail? No. We can be successful if we're prepared to ask for help.

> The number one thing we must do to grow spiritually is meet with God in and through His Word every day. There are no shortcuts.

Here's where the rubber hits the road: Bible engagement thrives when it's a mutual affair; specifically, when it's a partnership with God. Don't try to go it alone. The discipline of Bible reading, reflection, remembering and responding will blossom when you incline your heart to God (Proverbs 2:2), ask Him to fill you with the Holy Spirit (Ephesians 5:18), look to Him to renew your mind (Romans 12:2), and seek the kingdom of God and his righteousness (Matthew 6:33).

PRACTICES

In Section 2 you'll consider the practices involved in Bible engagement. The practices are the activities or methods that we use to connect with the Bible. As you explore this section you'll discover that we don't read the Bible like we read other books, that critical thinking about the Scriptures should be wed to sanctified imagination, that our study of the Bible is enhanced by contemplation and memorization, and much more.

Less is more when you read this section. Don't assume you should do everything that's mentioned. There are some things that everyone really should do, like listening (metaphorically) and interpreting, but other suggestions are optional, like journaling or singing, while still others, like preaching and teaching, are only applicable to some people.

Small chunks of reading are better than big chunks. This section is content-rich. It has lists of suggestions that, taken as a whole, may leave you wondering, "Where do I start?" So don't read this section in one sitting. Nibble away at it. And don't feel you have to act on every chapter and every idea, because if you do you may be overwhelmed. Rather, see this section as a toolbox of practices which you pick and choose from as the Spirit leads.

Another factor at play when you read this section is who you are. Your personality, learning mode, age, culture and denominational background significantly influence the way you engage with the Bible. For example, if you're an analytical person you'll have a natural bias for studying the Word, but you may dislike Lectio Divina. If you're a visually creative person you may enjoy journaling the Word and sharing your illustrative techniques on Instagram. And if you're a poet, spoken word may be a dynamic way for you to enact the Bible.

While you'll naturally have an affinity for some Bible engagement practices, you shouldn't ignore or dismiss the practices outside of your experience. Your Bible engagement can be enriched by new practices. So read this section with an openness to learning fresh ways to engage your senses with the Bible. And read this section appreciating how we all connect with the Bible differently.

Finally, one of the aims in this book is for each chapter to stand alone. Due to this endeavour you may experience a sense of déjà-vu as you digest this section. That's because there's intentional repetition to reinforce the basics, but with different levels of detail.

LISTENING

We are to hear. All of us are. That is what the whole Bible is calling out ... But hear what? The Bible is hundreds upon hundreds of voices all calling at once out of the past and clamouring for our attention ... And somewhere in the midst of them all one particular voice speaks out that is unlike any other voice because it speaks so directly to the deepest privacy and longing and weariness of each of us that there are times when the centuries are blown away like mist, and it is as if we stand with no shelter of time at all between ourselves and the one who speaks our secret name. Come, the voice says. Unto me. All ye. Every last one.

Frederick Buechner, "A Room Called Remember."

From the biblical perspective, engagement with God's Word primarily involves listening and hearing. The words "listen" and "hear" are found more than 1,500 times in the Bible. *"Turn your ear to my words,"* says the Lord (Proverbs 4:20).

God has much to say to us (Proverbs 4:20-22; Luke 11:28; Romans 10:17). In both the Old and New Testaments, God has spoken at many times and in many ways (Hebrews 1:1). But in order to hear what God says, we must know how to listen.

Listening to God's Word is not a straightforward affair. The kind of hearing God wants from us involves more than physical listening - it requires an act of faith. To really listen to God's Word we have to hear with faith (Galatians 3:2,5). Listening and faith are basic components of Bible engagement. *"Faith comes from hearing the message, and the message is heard through the word of Christ"* Romans 10:17.

> Listening and faith are basic components of Bible engagement.

In addition to faith, listening involves paying careful attention to what we hear (Mark 4:24) and how we hear (Luke 8:18). It also requires intentionality, effort, and discipline.

How to listen well

Here are 12 ways to cultivate good listening:

1. Incline your heart. Good listening begins with a humble heart. If our hearts are calloused they will be closed to what God has to say (Matthew 13:15). When our hearts are receptive they will receive God's Word and understand it (Matthew 13:23).

2. Prioritize your time. The death of Bible engagement begins when we think that our time is too valuable to spend listening to God.

3. Concentrate. To hear God we must, in many instances, listen for *"a gentle whisper"* 1 Kings 19:12. Distractions or peripheral thoughts can drown out or divert us from hearing what God is saying. To listen attentively to the Word we must turn off our smartphones and disengage from social media.

4. Focus on God. When we're preoccupied with ourselves, we listen poorly. We're more interested in what we have to say than in what God has to say. Good listening is intent on hearing and continuing to hear exclusively what God is saying to us.

5. Be aware of the enemy. Satan doesn't want us to listen to God. The powers in this dark world and the spiritual forces of evil (Ephesians 6:12) will do everything possible to drown out the voice of God.

6. Be patient. Learn to wait on God. Avoid listening half-heartedly and never assume you know what God has to say. According to Lutheran pastor and theologian, Dietrich Bonhoeffer, we should also avoid "an impatient, inattentive listening, that ... is only waiting for a chance to speak."

7. Pay attention to form and content. We need to know how to listen in order to effectively interpret the Scriptures. Scholar, author and poet Eugene Peterson says, "Listening requires listening to the way it is said (form) as well as to what is said (content)."

8. Let go of your ego. To listen well we need to be inwardly silent. Good listening can only happen when we ask God to separate us from our arrogance, wilfulness and self-assertiveness.

9. Cleanse your mind. Good listening requires a clear uncluttered mind. Diadochos of Photice, a 5th century writer, recommended the prayer "Lord Jesus Christ have mercy on me a sinner" as a way to cleanse and bind the mind.

10. Practice. In an age when talking prevails, listening needs to be practiced and learned. Real listening comes only as the consequence of training oneself to wait on God.

11. Be Christ-centred. Good listening is attentive to the Word of Christ. At the Transfiguration *"a voice from the cloud said, 'This is my Son, whom I love; with him I am well pleased. Listen to him!'"* Matthew 17:5.

12. Respond. Jesus repeatedly taught His disciples the importance of putting His words into practice (Luke 6:46-49; 8:21; 11:28). McKnight says, "God speaks to us for a reason ... so we can enter into a relationship with him, listen to him, and live out his Word in our day and in our way."

READING

The Bible needs a slower, smarter, deeper engagement ... eating good meals rather than speed snacking on what Philip Yancey calls "Scripture McNuggets."

Glenn R. Paauw, "Saving the Bible from Ourselves."

The Apostle Paul, in his instructions to Timothy, says, *"Focus on reading the Scriptures"* 1 Timothy 4:13 (NLT). It was excellent advice for Timothy and it's excellent advice for Christians. Reading the Bible should be for the Christian what eating and drinking is for the common person.

"One of the core reasons for our Bible engagement breakdown is that so many would-be Bible readers have been sold the mistaken notion that the Bible is a look-it-up-and-find-the-answer handy guide to life," says Glenn Paauw, the director of the Institute for Bible Reading. So what's involved with reading the Bible? Is it snacking on a verse a day, cherry picking the verses we like, digesting a book in one sitting, or something else?

While a verse a day has some value, it doesn't help Christians grow. A verse here and there simply cannot sustain us spiritually. Bible reading is about something more than a few, brief, preferred encounters with the Scriptures. It's about connecting on a deeper level through questioning, learning, understanding, growing, obeying, and living out the Scriptures. When Christians subsist on a diet of Scripture snacks, they're not feeding on the Word! Bible reading is more than a catchphrase, more than a short-lived inspirational text, and more than samplings of texts isolated from their historical, literary or cultural contexts.

Maybe one of the more recent reasons why Bible reading is sometimes equated with small readings is the influence of social media. Facebook, Snapchat, Twitter and texting are altering the way we read by hard-wiring our brains for sound-bites and little more. Studies suggest this influences how we interpret the Bible. When we read electronically it's a more flat, literal, information focused kind of reading that's less connected to broader themes and emotional content. The result, according to Pete Phillips, director of the Codec Research Centre for Digital Theology at Durham University in the UK, is that we "end up reading the text as though it was Wikipedia, rather than it being a sacred text in itself."

So what's involved in adequately reading the Bible? For starters, our Bible reading needs to be slower, smarter, sizeable and shared. Slower, because we need to soak in the Word. Smarter, because we need to dig into the Word. Sizeable, because we need to feed on the Word. And shared, because we need to teach one another the Word.

Reading the Bible should be like eating a good meal. While the size of our spiritual mouths and appetites will vary, our personal Bible reading should include daily readings from the Old or New Testament. To this end a good Bible reading guide (e.g. theStory™ - a free online resource from Scripture Union) is helpful because it facilitates Old and New Testament readings with reflections that help us enter into God's Story and find our part in it.

Bible reading needs to be slower, smarter, sizeable, and shared.

While it's good to read the Bible personally, we should also read it communally. A good meal is best eaten in the company of others. The Bible is first and foremost His Story, then our story, and finally, my story. So when we read the Bible we must also read it as members of a big family - as one of many listeners and participants (past and present).

Slower, smarter, sizeable and shared readings are necessary in order for the Bible to be a story we simmer in and a set of books we intimately know. That's not to say that we can fully digest what we read. Every word, sentence and paragraph of Scripture possess multiple relationships to the whole. Regardless of how much we read, we'll never fully plumb the depths of the Word.

PERSONAL READING

We must offer our discipline of spiritual reading to God with no strings attached, no demands, no limits, no expectations. We must offer it to God for God's purposes, allowing it to become a means of God's grace to transform our being.

Robert Mulholland, "Shaped by the Word."

We've all been taught how to read and we all read with similar preconditioned dynamics that are deeply ingrained in the way we read. Here's how it plays out:

"We come to a text with our own agenda firmly in place, perhaps not always consciously but usually unconsciously. If what we start to read does not fairly quickly begin to adapt itself to our agenda, we usually lay it aside and look for something that does. When what we are reading does adapt itself to our agenda, we then exercise control over it by grasping it with our mind. The rational, cognitive, intellectual dynamics of our being go into full operation to analyze, critique, dissect, reorganize, synthesize, and digest the material we find appropriate to our agenda. Thus our general mode of reading is to perceive the text as an object 'out there' over which we have control. We control our approach to the text; we control our interaction with the text; we control the impact of the text upon our lives," says professor and author, Robert Mulholland.

To summarize, the way we read is based on three ingrained assumptions:

- We are the masters of what we read.
- Texts/content are subordinate to our intellect.
- We have the right to choose what to do or not do with what we learn.

When it comes to Bible reading, these assumptions create tremendous obstacles. Here's why: The author of the Bible, God, is all-knowing, all-wise, and all-powerful. *"'For my thoughts are not your thoughts, neither are your ways my ways,' declares the Lord. 'As the heavens are higher than the earth, so are my ways higher than your ways and my thoughts than your thoughts'"* Isaiah 55:8-9. That places God in control, not us.

> When we read the Word we cannot, and should not, be masters of what we read.

Because God is in control, we must come under the authority of His Word. That is, we must read the Bible on its own terms. When we read the Word we cannot, and should not, be the masters of what we read. Nor can we stand to one side exercising our cognition and intellect to evaluate the text in the light of our own best interests. Rather, the Bible must read us!

So how do we read the Bible without controlling the text, our interaction with the text, and the impact of the text on our lives? Through the cultivation of humility, by learning how to listen, by inclining our hearts, and by being soul aware.

Humble yourself. Reading begins with the right approach. "The beginning of good Bible engagement is a bit of reflection on what it means to be a virtuous reader in general," says Paauw. Because God is omniscient, because His Word is holy, and because He's God (and we're not), being humble is the only acceptable way for us to read His Word. Humility is a bankruptcy of spirit (Matthew 5:3). It's depending solely on God's righteousness (Luke 18:9-14). It's receiving something from God like a little child (Luke 18:15-17). And it's tied up with fearing the Lord (Psalm 25:9-12; Proverbs 15:33). Now here's the kicker: We need humility to read the Bible because without it we lack wisdom (Proverbs 11:2). When we don't have wisdom the Bible is confusing; we don't know how to hear or understand God's Word (Matthew 13:13).

Learn to listen. There are two types of listening: the everyday superficial kind of listening and the listening that happens (when we are patient and still - Psalm 37:7) in the depths of our being. We need to learn to listen from the inner reaches of who we are - to pay attention not just with our minds, but with our hearts and spirits. For this kind of listening to take place, we must focus all our faculties on God. We must hear and see beyond the words on the page to find and know the God who "speaks" those words. And when we find Him, we must open our ears and receive instruction, comfort, renewal, grace, rebuke, correction, or whatever He wants to share with us.

Incline your heart. *"Trust in the Lord with all your heart and lean not on your own understanding"* Proverbs 3:5. Biblically speaking, the heart is the centre of our emotional, intellectual and moral activity. It's the inner sanctum where the experiences of joy, sorrow, love, fear and the whole range of emotions occur. The emotional state of the heart impacts our whole being (Proverbs 15:13; 17:22). It's also the wellspring of our hopes and desires. Most importantly, when we look for God with all our heart, that's when we find Him (Deuteronomy 4:28-29).

Be soul-aware. When we read and hear the Scriptures rationally and critically there's a tendency (and danger) to manipulate the text to validate the pervasive make-up of our self-referenced being. To counteract this tendency we need to be soul-aware. The road to being soul-aware begins with dying to self and denying *"the desires of the sinful nature"* Galatians 5:16. It's also letting our response to God's Word percolate into the core of our volitional nature. This is done, in part, through asking questions like, "What am I feeling?" or "What is God stirring up in me?" or "How is the Spirit moving my spirit?"

> When we read the Bible the right way the Spirit who inspired the Scriptures also inspires our reading of the Scriptures.

Medieval German monk and writer Thomas à Kempis said, "A humble knowledge of ourselves is a surer way to God than is the search for depth of learning." So let's not read the Bible the way we've been taught to read other books. We cannot and should not take control of the text as if it's powerless without our intervention. That's a sure-fire way to filter out God's voice! Let's read it in a new way. Let's read it without "reading" it. Let's read it with what the ancient writers called "Holy Expectancy."

That is, read it with vulnerability - with a desire to hear, be transformed, and obey it.

If reading the Bible without "reading" it sounds intimidating, here's a word of encouragement: When we read the Bible the right way, the living Author joins us. We don't do it in our own strength and it's not a one-sided enterprise. The Spirit who inspired the Scriptures also inspires our reading of the Scriptures by "opening up" the Scriptures so we can see Jesus.

COMMUNAL READING

Wherever we are located within that all-inclusive community, we have the great privilege of seeing the Scripture through the eyes of the whole community ... How boring life would be if we listened only to our own insights! How narrow our vision would be if we limited it only to our own understanding! How sad it would be if we missed out on what God has for all of us by failing to listen to how God speaks at various times and in various ways through parts of the whole.

Richard J. Foster.

A highlight of my early adulthood was lying on the campus lawns at the Johannesburg College of Education while reading and discussing the Scriptures with Christian friends. Uniquely, we had no program, no leaders' guide and no set time for our meetings. No one told us to do it. We simply had a desire to get together, open the Scriptures and read them. It was organic, compelling and Spirit empowered. It often lasted for a few hours and we'd usually read a whole book in one sitting (we chose the shorter ones). To this day I fondly remember our lively debates and deliberations during the reading of Hosea.

One of the characteristics of the church should be community. Yet individualism, deeply entrenched in the church because of the influence of Western culture, has resulted in a strong person-centred approach to Bible reading, particularly among Evangelicals. Many of us read the Bible privately, but that shouldn't be the only way we do it. Bible reading is deficient when it's exclusive, yet blossoms when done in community. This shouldn't surprise us. God is shaping each one of us as a person, but more importantly He is calling, gathering and forming us as a people. We're in Christ together. That's why life with God, by definition, is life shared with God's people.

Ways to read in community

So when, how and where do we read the Bible in community? Here are 10 suggestions:

1. Read at the dinner table. God placed us in families. The starting place for reading the Bible in community should be the home.

2. Read in different settings. Read the Bible in church services, in small life groups, and (when permitted) in public settings.

3. Read the Bible as a summons to assemble together. When we gather to worship, the Bible should be read "not as information, not just as instruction, but as a summons to assemble together" says the Welsh theologian and poet, Rowan Williams.

4. Read the Bible to talk about it. There are three factors, according to the Canadian Bible Engagement Study (CBES), that drive Bible reading: confidence, conversation and community. Rick Hiemstra, director of research at the Evangelical Fellowship of Canada, says, "Reflection on the meaning of the Bible for people's lives is an important kind of Bible engagement, but conversation with others about the meaning of the Bible is the key factor in deepening Bible engagement."

> Bible reading is deficient when it's exclusive, yet blossoms when done in community.

5. Read to be faithful to it. Bonhoeffer, the Lutheran pastor who opposed Nazi ideology and was executed by the Nazis in 1945, recognized that we must be "willing to allow the present age in general, and our lives in particular, to be interrogated by the Scriptures. The German Christians only read the Bible for themselves, discarding what they didn't want. But the call is to read Scripture over-against ourselves, allowing Scripture to question our lives."

6. Read prayerfully. When we pray before, after, or even during the communal reading of the Scriptures, we acknowledge that we're reading the living Word of God and indicating to everyone present that reading the Bible isn't an end in itself.

7. Read the Bible thinking about one another. "Read the Bible through the lens of others' experiences, in the knowledge of others' stories, in the midst of immersion in others' lives," suggests Richard Foster, a Quaker writer and spirituality teacher.

8. Read to spur one another on. *"And let us consider how we may spur one another on toward love and good deeds, not giving up meeting together, as some are in the habit of doing, but encouraging one another—and all the more as you see the Day approaching"* Hebrews 10:24-25.

9. Read the Bible to proclaim God's mighty acts. *"But you are a chosen people, a royal priesthood, a holy nation, God's special possession, that you may declare the praises of him who called you out of darkness into his wonderful light"* 1 Peter 2:9.

10. Read inclusively. The Bible is our common text. We should read it in a spirit of unity embracing every ethnicity, every generation and every tradition.

Of course it should go without saying that when we read the Bible in community we should always do so in a way that leads us to Christ and ends in holy compliance. This cannot be emphasized enough. When communal Bible reading is Christ-centred the community will know how to take part in the reality of which the Scriptures speak.

PUBLIC READING

Scripture must be central to our worship services. We ought to read it, sing it and preach it every Sunday! Reading Scripture is not something we do out of duty or obligation, but something we do in delight, trusting that it is a means by which the Lord blesses pursues, convicts and draws. To stand at the front of a church and read the Bible is to stand in the place of God and proclaim his Word.

Tim Challies, "The Public Reading of Scripture."

In an average church service on an average Sunday we often hear an average reading of God's Word. It's heartbreaking. Lacklustre public reading of the Scriptures is a discredit to God's people and a slight to God! An average reading of God's Word isn't good enough. We should never read the Bible in a boring, nondescript, half-baked way.

When we read the Bible publicly we should read it well - very well! It is, after all, God's Word. And God's Word, invested with the life giving power of His Spirit, is dynamic, transformational and alive. So let's read it publicly like we believe it. Let's read it energetically, passionately, thoughtfully, dramatically, inspirationally, and motivationally. Let's read it like it's coursing through our veins and pounding in our hearts.

To get the full force of God's Word we must revive its spoken nature. From its inception the Bible was given to us to be read aloud and heard (Nehemiah 8, Psalm 119:13, Revelation 1:3). So how do we devote ourselves to the public reading of Scripture (1 Timothy 4:13)?

> To get the full force of God's Word we must revive its spoken nature.

Tips for public reading of Scripture

Here are some pointers:
- Start by understanding the passage.
- Know how to pronounce names of people and places.
- Prepare, practice and pray.
- Prepare a script (print out a copy in a large font, break up the text, mark where you take a breath).
- Identify who is speaking.
- Become the character.
- Help the listener hear it for the first time.
- Read from your heart and then from your lips.
- Convey the meaning of the words (not just the sounds).
- Use pauses and break up the text so that it's easy to hear.
- Highlight the meaning of a text through tone, modulation and emphasis.
- Read dynamically (the Bible is not a telephone directory!).
- Bring freshness and vitality.
- Let the text inform how you read it.

And here are some common mistakes that should be avoided:

- Inadequate preparation.
- Reading too slow or too fast .
- Using a sing-song or preacher voice.
- Speaking too loud or too soft.
- Reading in a monotone.
- No feeling or too much feeling.
- Trailing off with words or sentences.
- Not looking up (use a music stand, pulpit or lectern to get the right height).
- Not reading like a town-crier.
- Not reading with passion.

There's awesome power in God's spoken Word. When we read the Bible publicly we should read it like we're hearing it for the first time. We should read the Scriptures believing that they'll bring salvation, comfort, understanding, discomfort, remorse, joy and all manner of life-changing encounters with the living God.

Humdrum public reading of the Word should be anathema. Yes, we're inadequate when it comes to reading the Word as it should be read, but God's grace is sufficient for everything we do. So we must ask God to empower us in our weakness, then read His Word with stirring voices and enthusiasm, expecting God to engage people's hearts, minds, wills and souls.

READING METHODS

One of the great problems in Bible reading is that we move our eyes over the words and come to the end of a column and don't know what we've read; we don't feel our minds or spirits expanded because we saw nothing fresh. It was purely mechanical. There was no discovery, no life, and no breakthroughs to new insight. One of the best ways to change that is to train yourself to ask questions of the text. Often the posing of the question itself will already carry its answer with it and will open your mind to new things.

John Piper, "The Baptism and the Genealogy of Jesus."

If we don't have a regular intake of God's Word we can't grow in our engagement with the Bible. The common denominator for every healthy growing Christian is that they're spending consistent regular time reading, reflecting, remembering and responding to God's Word. To do this effectively we need a solid Bible reading method.

There are many different methods for reading the Bible. In his book, "Learn To Study The Bible," Andy Deane discusses 40 different step-by-step methods, several of which are designed for children, including "Heart Monitor," "Funnel It," "Weather Report," "Climb the Ladder," or "Cross Thoughts."

Before looking at three different reading methods for adults, we should note that every method presupposes two things. First, we should put aside time every day to read the Word. Bible reading should be a regular and consistent practice. For a morning person like me, the best time of the day for Bible reading is before anyone else in the house is up and about. Second, we must try to eliminate distractions. Mulholland identifies the importance of being "outwardly" and "inwardly" unhindered as "a time when you can center down or be still and open to God alone."

With the above in mind, here are three valuable methods to consider:

Manuscript Method

> "Biblical studies can be overwhelming. Words like exegesis and hermeneutics are tossed into the fray and it can feel like you need a seminary degree just to stay afloat. But luckily, you don't need a Ph.D. in biblical studies to glean meaning and application from Scripture. All you need is a Bible and the willingness to ask the right questions. The trick is to think inductively. If you pay attention to the details—the who, what, when, where, and most importantly, the why - then you have all you need to let the Holy Spirit bring the text to life."

Justin Marr, "Dig Deep Into God's Word."

The manuscript method (also known as the Inductive Bible Study method) involves observation, interpretation and application. It begins with a passage of Scripture prepared on a document with the chapter and verse numbers, paragraph headings and footnotes removed. Only the words of Scripture remain in the document. One then uses different coloured pens, highlighters or pencils to circle, underline, connect, draw symbols (e.g. lightning bolt for judgment, heart for love) and generally mark up the passage. The manuscript method is great for private or communal Bible reading.

With a pen or highlighter in hand, the method involves the following:

Pray. Invite the Holy Spirit to guide and direct your study of the text.

Ask the big six questions. Keep on asking who, why, what, where, how and what's that doing there? [These questions are dealt with in more detail in the chapter on "Analyzing."]

Identify key words and phrases. Key words or phrases convey the author's point or purpose for writing. Underline or highlight them.

List and number. List what you learn or number connected items in the text.

Compare and contrast. Evaluate differences, measure and match up, consider similarities.

Time changes. Sequences of time and events provide clues to help understand the text.

Location. Where is the event happening?

Opening and closing phrases. Pay attention to words and phrases like "when," "then," "the next day," "therefore," "thus," "for this reason," etc.

Identify people. Who is involved or mentioned and how do they relate to one another?

Discover the theme. What is the main idea or teaching? What title would you give to the text?

Share and apply. Discuss your findings with others. Live out what you've learnt.

Scripture Union Method

"Think of your Bible reading and prayer as interaction with God, as a meeting, not just a habit. Of course, a regular quiet time requires some discipline. But the main motivation is not to keep up with anything, or earn anything, or prove anything. It's about spending quality time with the One who made you, knows you, and loves you. If you will begin consciously approaching your Bible reading and prayer as dialog with God, "the waiting Father," as Theologian Helmut Thielicke described him, the issue will no longer be guilt, but love."

Whitney T. Kuniholm, "Confessions of a Guilty Bible Reader."

For many decades people throughout the world have found the Scripture Union Method to be of great benefit in helping them meet with God daily and live out His Story. Scripture Union's Bible reading guides for all ages enable people to read and reflect on a 10 to 20 verse passage each day in order to go through the whole Bible in about five years. The method involves the following:

Pray that God will help you understand what you're about to read. Ask Him for insight.

Read carefully through the passage.

Think about what you've read, using these questions to guide you:
- What does the passage teach about the Father, Son, or Holy Spirit?
- What is the main lesson for me today? What is the main verse to think about? Underline the verse or memorize it.
- Read through the Scripture Union guide for additional help in understanding the passage.

Apply what you've learned.

Pray using the thoughts and insights you've gained from your reading and reflection. Ask God to help you live out your faith today.

LM's Method

"I study my Bible as I gather apples. I shake the Bible as a whole, like shaking the whole tree. Then I shake every limb - study book after book. Then I shake every branch, giving attention to the chapters when they do not break the sense. Then I shake every twig, or a careful study of the paragraphs and sentences and words and their meanings."

Martin Luther.

Here's a tried and tested method for reading and reflecting on God's Word that I developed for myself as a young adult:

Prepare. Thank God for the opportunity to meet with Him. Ask forgiveness for sins of omission or commission.

Perimeter. Look at the passage in context and study what comes before and after the text you're reading. Avoid reading anything into the passage that may distort the intended meaning.

Paraphrase. Write out the passage using words that would enable a child to understand it.

Pulverize. Ponder on every phrase and sentence. Find the main point. Look at opening and closing statements. Identify unique words, locate points of emphasis, and pay attention to historical, cultural, social, political, or economic factors.

Personalize. Apply the passage to yourself. Be an open-hearted recipient. Be aware of the paralysis of analysis (don't become a critical analyst of God's Word). Ask yourself, "What does God want me to learn?" and "How does God want me to respond?" Think about how the passage helps you know Christ and makes Him known.

Praise. Give God the honour and glory that He deserves.

Prayer. Pray using the passage as the point of departure. Repeat the Word back to God. Ask God to help you be obedient to His Word.

Practice. Act on what you learnt from God today. Share biblical insights with friends and family.

Here's an important caveat concerning Bible reading: Bible reading isn't an end in itself. We read the Bible as a means to an end - and that end is to see and know the Person behind the text (John 6:35). "Reading the Bible as Scripture is never a matter of handling texts and the relationship between texts. It is above all a matter of being in the presence and open to the handling of the One who ... is the final Author of its message, because he is the One whose story it tells, and it is as we know him, as we dwell in his presence, and as he dwells in us that we see and hear what he is saying and showing us through it," says theologian and teacher Trevor Hart.

All told, a good Bible reading method must lead us to the place where we're like-minded, have the same love, are one in spirit, and of one mind with Christ (Philippians 2:1-4). So if a Bible reading method doesn't help us find life and fullness of life in Christ (John 10:10), then the method is deficient.

> We read the Bible as a means to an end - and that end is to see and know the Person behind the text.

SYNTHESIZING

The challenge - never negligible - regarding the Christian Scriptures is getting them read, but read on their own terms, as God's revelation.

Eugene Peterson, "Eat This Book."

Reading or hearing the Bible should be more than the bare necessities that are easily digested in two minutes. Scripture should be read holistically. When we read the Bible we should read it as it was written - by individual books. We must read texts in their contexts and stories within the framework of the grand Story. Why? Because the meaning of the texts and stories are accurately gleaned only when we read with a clear understanding of the larger context, sub-themes of the books, and theme of the Bible as a whole.

"We will gain a much better understanding of what the Bible is all about if we stand back and take a look at the whole. Move too quickly to the detail and we may well find the passage that we are reading doesn't make a lot of sense. Worse, it may seem to make sense but we may have missed the real significance, or even misunderstood," says theological consultant and writer, John Grayston.

God speaks to us through His Word. When texts or stories are read in isolation they can be interpreted with meaning they were never meant to convey. God wants us to know truth. When we de-contextualize Scripture or read passages divorced from the overarching narrative we may get lost in a web of details, or worse, overlook what God is really saying.

One of the requirements for the seminary students in my class, "Bible Engagement - Encountering the Bible in a Life Changing Way," is to read the book of Titus once through, every day, for seven consecutive days. They must read it in the same version, without the use of commentaries or guides, uninfluenced by chapter or verse designations, and in prayerful reliance on the Holy Spirit.

> When texts or stories are read in isolation they can be interpreted with meaning they were never meant to convey.

Reading each book of the Bible as a whole is called the synthetic study of the Bible (it has similarities to Lectio Continua, i.e., continuous reading). It's so named because it majors on synthesis (combining into a coherent whole, putting together) as distinct from analysis (separating into constituent elements, taking apart).

The method is straightforward: A book of the Bible is read through in one sitting, repeatedly, independently (with no study aids) and continuously (daily for 15 to 30 days), until one has a thorough grasp of the outline and sub-themes. It's a "big-picture" reading of the Bible that happens when we intentionally ignore the details. In other words, it's not about inspecting each tree in the forest; it's about viewing the forest from above and seeing how the trees are an interconnected ecosystem.

The synthetic study of the Bible has many benefits: It helps us experience the force of the book in its entirety, builds understanding of a book as it relates to the other books of the Bible and helps us see important themes. It develops interpretive skills, enlarges mental vision, strengthens faith, and compels us to rely on the Holy Spirit for insight and understanding. Because it majors on repetition it helps us remember the text, which in turn fuels introspection that leads to conviction, prayer and life change. It also helps us see "the beauty of the whole forest" and thereby enables us to come to know Christ better.

Wayne Davies, president of Good Messengers Ministries, wanted to read the Bible in a way that would help him become much more familiar with it. He started reading the shorter books of the New Testament repeatedly, in one sitting. It revolutionized his Bible engagement. As he said, "I was blown away by the impact it had on my understanding. It really worked!"

How to do a synthetic study

The method, with pencil or pen in hand to make notes, is to read the book a few times in order to:

1. Discover the theme.
2. Identify the writer's purpose or goal.
3. See how the book is put together.
4. Enter into the emotion(s) of the book.
5. Get an all-encompassing picture of the book.

Then, as the big-picture comes into focus, identify:
1. The natural divisions in the book.
2. The genre(s) of literature.
3. The progression of the narrative.
4. The key facts.
5. How Christ is embedded in the book.

When you complete a synthetic reading, develop a book outline or summary that encapsulates your observations, identifies the main divisions and themes, and takes hold of how the overall message leads to Christ.

ANALYZING

*If the Bible is indeed God's Word written, we should
spare no pains and grudge no effort to discover
what he has said (and says) in Scripture.*

John R.W. Stott, "Understanding the Bible."

A good detective leaves no stone unturned in his or her hunt
for clues. Similarly, when we study the Bible we must do so
with attention to detail. Analysis is seeing the trees, not the
forest. It's separating the text into constituent elements -
breaking down the whole to see every part.

In analyzing a passage we must examine opening and closing
statements, find the key words and phrases, track repeated
words, analyze the grammar and sentence construction,
identify anomalies and paradoxes, look for comparisons and
contrast, classify the literary form, take note of the verbs,
see if there is anything unusual or unexpected, pigeonhole
any promises or commands, look for lists, chart general and
specific progressions, look for admonitions and instructions,
look for links to other verses of scripture, and look for Christ.

The ability to ask good questions is the essence of analysis.
Bible engagement is strengthened when we intensely and

systematically dig into God's Word by asking probing questions. No question should be off-limits. The American author J. R. Briggs says that asking questions is "the secret sauce of Scripture engagement ... asking engaging questions, or even frustrating, scary questions, that's where we really start to learn."

The key to good analysis "and therefore to a more intelligent reading of the Bible, is to learn to read the text carefully and to ask the right questions of the text," say professors Gordon D. Fee and Douglas Stuart.

The big six questions

According to writer and IT project manager Henry Jackson, there are six essential questions that should be asked of the text in order to reveal its meaning:

1. Who is speaking? To whom and about whom is the passage speaking? Who wrote the passage? Who are the main characters? Who else is mentioned in the book?

2. What is the author doing? What are the main events? What are the circumstances? What are the main ideas? What is the historical or cultural setting (as determined from the text)? What is the genre of the passage? What is the theme of the chapter or book?

3. Why was this written? Why is a particular thing said? Why is he/she in a certain place?

4. Where did (or will) this happen? Where was this book/passage written or said? Where did the main events of the passage take place?

5. When was this written (on the biblical history timeline)? When was the passage written during the authors life? When did (or will) this happen? When did the author say/do it?

6. How will (or did) something happen? How is the truth illustrated? How did the passage/letter/book/message affect people?

> Bible engagement is strengthened by asking probing questions.

Analyzing a passage takes time and requires repeated reading. This is because a good analysis requires an in-depth understanding of the theme, discovering what it says about Christ, studying the people involved, identifying key verses, recognizing the central lesson, looking for promises to be received, determining what commands need to be acted on, finding out if there are mistakes to be avoided, and seeing if there are examples to follow.

STUDYING

If you want to understand the Scripture in the Spirit in which it is written, you have to attend to the content and to the unity of Scripture as a whole.

Joseph Ratzinger, "Jesus of Nazareth."

Most people say they study the Bible for one or more of the following reasons:

For information or knowledge. There's a natural desire to understand the Bible. People study the Bible to gather facts, learn doctrinal truths, build a set of beliefs, or understand historical events. But God's Word wasn't primarily given to us for this purpose. It's not what Foster disparagingly refers to as the definitive "Field Guide to Faith." We should never study the Bible as detached historians or ivory tower academics. If the sole objective for studying the Bible is for gaining knowledge, then the outcome will be pride (1 Corinthians 8:1).

To be biblically literate. Another motivation for studying the Bible is to be familiar with it. The goal of biblical literacy is biblical competence. But God's Word wasn't given to us so that we could master it. Studying the Bible for the sole purpose of being biblically proficient is a self-serving objective.

For answers to pressing needs. Because we're human our needs are understandably important. Problems with our health, financial issues, matters involving our sexuality, how to find forgiveness, guidance for work and family issues, and so much more, are the everyday realities of life. But as biblical scholar and professor Mark Strauss says, the Bible "is not a 'magic-answer' book for decision making in life." Nor is it primarily given to us to figure out how we can be good financial managers, loving spouses, or victorious Christians. If the sole objective for studying the Bible is to find answers to our pressing needs, then we'll end up controlling the Bible rather than allowing the Bible to control us.

> If the sole objective for studying the Bible is for gaining knowledge, then the outcome will be pride.

So why should we study the Bible if it's not primarily for information or knowledge, to be biblically literate, or to find answers for our pressing needs?

The principal reason why we study the Bible should be to know Christ and the abundant life that comes from Him. The aim isn't external conformity; it's internal transformation (Psalm 51:6, 10). Study the Bible to learn how to *"Love the Lord your God with all your heart and with all your soul and with all your mind. This is the first and greatest commandment,"* Matthew 22:37-38. What follows is *"Love your neighbour as yourself,"* Matthew 22:39. If we study the Bible to figure out how to love ourselves first and then love God, we've put the cart before the horse. We study the Bible to love Christ and then, out of a place of intimacy with Christ, we study the Bible to learn how to love others and ourselves.

Regarding our study of the Bible, "perhaps the most basic question is: Shall we try to control the Bible, that is, try to make it 'come out right,' or shall we simply seek to release its life into our lives and into the world? Shall we try to 'tilt' it this way or that, or shall we give it complete freedom to 'tilt' us as it will," says Foster.

With Foster's questions in mind, how then do we study the Bible in a way that allows the Bible to have its way with us?

How to study the Bible

Here are 10 suggestions:

1. Savour the Word through formative listening, reading, and contemplation. To study the Bible effectively we must experience God's Word personally by immersing both our heads and hearts in the text. All our senses should be engaged with one intent - to receive from Him. Peterson says, "Exegesis is loving God enough to stop and listen carefully to what he says." We mustn't rush - the more time we spend in brooding consideration of the text, the more likely it will be for the Bible to have its way with us.

2. Investigate the text's reality and power. Professor and itinerant preacher Michael Quicke refers to this process as "swimming in its currents." In recognizing that quality exegesis requires both "participation and immersion," Quicke says, "Committed exegetes explore both with an openness, like curious children awakened to something they do not know yet, and with mature reflection that discerns what God may be saying."

3. Don't try to fit the Bible into theological or doctrinal boxes. The aim is not doctrinal certainty or saying everything we can possibly say about a passage. We obscure the purpose of Scripture if we dissect and organize it like a laboratory specimen. If our tendency, when studying the Word, is to flatten it out, manage it, trivialize it, diminish it, or render it inane, then "our technical way of thinking reduces mystery to problem, transforms assurance into certitude, revises quality into quantity, and so takes the categories of biblical faith and represents them in manageable shapes," explains American theologian Walter Brueggemann. Or worse, if we study the Bible in a way in which "the Scriptures are treated as just another tool for enlightenment or access to knowledge that is power, sacrilege has been committed," says Peterson.

4. Study the Bible through a Christ-centred lens. Bible study is always about ultimately understanding the story of following Jesus. Effective Bible study therefore requires an in-depth investigation of how Christ is implicitly or explicitly woven through the text.

5. Don't privatize the Bible. There's a place for individual study of the Bible, but not for individualistic study of the Bible. God's Word is not owned by us and should not be controlled by us. We should neither possess nor isolate Scripture for our own ends. If our study of the Bible is focused on how we can "name it and claim it," we've erred. If our study of the Bible is viewed through a grid of financial blessing and physical well-being, we've erred. If our study of the Bible is to fashion an individualized faith or religious experience, we've erred. Peterson aptly notes, "When we privatize Scripture we embezzle the common currency of God's revelation."

6. Know that all Scripture is set in story. The prayers, poems, hymns, letters, chronicles, prophecies, teachings, genealogies, proverbs and such are all individual forms within a larger narrative that gives the individual forms their coherency. Thus to study the Bible in a way that disconnects it from its overarching narrative form will change or distort the content.

7. Evaluate what the preaching professor Thomas Long refers to as the "focus" and "function" of the text. Focus describes what the text is saying and function describes what the text is doing. What the text intends to say and do becomes the "compass settings" for what we must say and do.

8. Be irrepressibly curious and interested in everything. We must exercise our powers of observation by paying attention to the details. We do this, not by taking charge of the text, but by entering the realm of the text and searching for what may be hidden.

9. Wait to consult biblical commentaries. Only use theological sources after doing everything that's already been mentioned (that said, it's helpful to understand the context of a text by first reading some historical and cultural study notes). This requires patience and courage. The tendency when studying a text is to get the experts' books in our hands as soon as possible. That's because we feel vulnerable without them. But if we go straight to commentaries, our study of the Bible becomes subject to someone else's study of the Bible. By leaving this step to the end you'll be more open to letting the Bible have its way with you.

10. Study the Bible with the intent to obey it. The Bible has only tilted "us as it will" when we put it into practice. "Obedience remains the true test of genuine faith," says Pope. Our Bible study has taken hold of us when we've been enlisted to follow Christ. The most important outcome when we study the Bible shouldn't be how much we've learnt; it should be how we're imitating Christ's humility every day (Philippians 2:1-11).

INTERPRETING

*The Bible contains its own hermeneutic ... In a
word, Jesus is the thread that holds all Scripture
together ... The Bible has no real meaning unless it
is grounded in Christ.*

Leonard Sweet and Frank Viola, "Jesus: A Theography."

A basic understanding of how to interpret God's Word is
essential to Bible engagement. The Bible must be unpacked
carefully and correctly, not sloppily or hastily. For, as the well
known theologian J. I. Packer wisely says, "A misinterpreted
Bible is a misunderstood Bible, which will lead us out of God's
way rather than in it."

Interpreting the Bible begins with knowing that each
verse in its context does not have multiple meanings (though
there may be multiple applications). God never intended for
the Scriptures to mean different things to different people
(nations, races, or cultural groups). There is one Author,
with one message and one meaning. That's not to say that the
message isn't multi-faceted, because it is. And it's not to say
that the meaning isn't nuanced, because it is. But it is to say

that our interpretation of the Bible must be consistent with God's intended message and meaning.

The Bible is a big sprawling story. Sometimes we forget that the Bible is first and foremost a story. Three-quarters of it is narrative and another 15 percent is poetry. Only about 10 percent consists of direct doctrinal teaching. Interpretation must therefore major on understanding the Bible as story. "It is vital that we understand scripture, and our relation to it, in terms of some kind of overarching narrative which makes sense of the texts. We cannot reduce scripture to a set of 'timeless truths' on the one hand, or to being merely the fuel for devotions on the other, without being deeply disloyal, at a structural level, to scripture itself," says Wright.

> Our interpretation of the Bible must be consistent with God's intended message and meaning.

The narrative nature of the Bible cannot be emphasized enough. "The Bible ... is not simply a collection of 'Sayings from Chairman God,'" say Fee and Stuart. If we think interpretation is about a set of propositions to be believed, or commands to be obeyed, we do God's Word (and ourselves) a horrible disservice. Principles and rules will not transform us. But encounters with the Author of the Story will.

So how do we interpret the Bible accurately, ensuring it's not just our opinion? How do we avoid distorting Scripture to our own destruction (2 Peter 3:16)? What are the basic hermeneutical guidelines? We begin with three teachers, three principles, three questions and three rules (gleaned from Alex Goodwin from the Institute of Bible Reading, Stott, Fee and Stuart):

Hermeneutical guidelines

Three Teachers

1. The Holy Spirit. The best interpreter of any book is its author. The Holy Spirit is the only One who reveals and illuminates truth (Psalm 119:18, 1 Corinthians 2:14, Matthew 11:25-25).

2. The Church. God reveals truth (from the past to the present) to and through the community of faith (Ephesians 3:18-19, Colossians 3:16).

3. Personal Study. We must also teach ourselves, yet do so in full dependence and humble submission to the Holy Spirit (Luke 12:57, 1 Corinthians 2:14-16, 10:15, 2 Timothy 2:7).

Three Principles

1. Natural Sense (the principle of simplicity). Look first for the obvious and natural meaning of the text, whether figurative or literal. Consider the intention of the writer or speaker.

2. Original Sense (the principle of history). The message of Scripture can only be understood as it relates to the circumstances in which it was originally written.

3. General Sense (the principle of harmony). There is an organic unity to the Bible. Approach the Scripture believing that God doesn't contradict Himself.

Three Questions

1. What did it mean to the original audience? Reading the Bible is a cross-cultural activity. The Bible was written for us, but not originally to us. Pay attention to the first "life-setting."

2. What type of literature is it? Each genre of biblical literature must be interpreted on its own terms (the different genres of literature in the Bible include history, narrative, wisdom literature, poetry, prophecy, apocalyptic, law, parables, gospels and letters/epistles).

3. Where does it fit in the Bible's overall story? Read with the big story in mind. Track the trajectory of the passage in relation to the major "acts" within the "drama."

Three Rules

1. Use several good translations. Don't be restricted or bound to the exegetical choices of a single translation.

2. Preserve the original intent of the text. A passage of Scripture cannot hold a different meaning than that which was held by the original human author or his readers.

3. Identify what's common. God's Word to us is the same as it was to those who first heard it, particularly when we share similar life situations.

Process of interpretation

With these guidelines in mind, how do we plainly and simply go about the task of understanding and explaining the Word of God (2 Timothy 2:15)? Here's a thumbnail sketch:

Pray fervently. The Holy Spirit is the One who reveals and illuminates truth (John 16:13). We need Him to interpret His Word. Without Him we lack understanding (1 Corinthians 2:14). As we seek to understand and apply the Bible, prayer should be interlaced throughout the process.

Be aware of your own presuppositions. Each of us comes to the Bible with a particular worldview and filter what we're reading through a series of cultural, theological and educational lenses. Theology professor J. Todd Billings says, "All interpretation is shaped, whether or not we recognize it or not, by the cultural context and social location of the interpreter." As such, it's impossible for anyone to have a neutral view of God's Word. To interpret the Word with integrity we must listen and seek to understand how other people interact with the Bible.

Use several translations. English Bibles are translations from Aramaic, Hebrew and Greek documents. Different translation philosophies (formal equivalence/word for word, dynamic equivalence/thought for thought) result in slightly different renderings of a text. Due to textual variants in the ancient manuscripts we should glean from a variety of translations and not be limited by the exegetical choices of a translation. Consider using the New International Version (NIV), New Living Translation (NLT), New Revised Standard Version

(NRSV), English Standard Version (ESV), Good News Bible (GNB), and the Message (MSG).

Check out the writer. To understand a text we need to know what the writer wanted his readers to gather from his words. Ask these questions: Who wrote the book? Where was he? When did he write it? Why did he write it? To whom did he write it?

Examine the setting. Analyze the place, plot and characters in the text. To discern how the original audience understood what was written to them requires a basic knowledge of their geographical location, history, politics, customs and culture.

Look at the immediate context. Texts in isolation from their context can be manipulated to say almost anything we want them to say, or be applied in ways that aren't true to the story as a whole. Read what precedes and follows the text in order to see how its content relates to the text you're studying.

Investigate the book context. The meaning of a text flows out of its broader framework. Understand the purpose, theme(s), section/divisions and flow of thought in the whole book. Ask, "Why did the human author write this book?" and "How should the text be understood in the light of the purpose and sub-themes of the book?"

Give thought to the whole-Bible context. Explore the wide-screen perspective. "It takes the whole Bible to read any part of the Bible," says Peterson. Author and photographer John Cross adds, "that to understand the Bible accurately, the biblical pieces must be put together in the right way." To do this we should ask, "How does the text fit into the bigger narrative?" Aim to compare scripture with scripture. Foster says we should "read the Bible in conversation with itself." Look for cross-references (other texts that relate to the text being studied). In due course the Bible should expound itself (Psalm 36:9).

Be aware of the literary genre. Different literary genres of Scripture have unique characteristics. For example, Hebrew poetry uses parallelism (the use of synonyms and antonyms to build ideas around other ideas) instead of rhyme.

Identify figurative language. The Bible uses both literal (words and phrases used according to their proper meaning or precise definition) and figurative (words and phrases that are not literal) language. There are more than a dozen different types of figurative language used in the Bible (e.g. allegory, hyperbole, anthropomorphism, metaphor, personification). To interpret figurative language literally, or literal language figuratively, will corrupt the meaning of the text.

Do word studies. Words are the basic building blocks of the Scriptures. Explore the close-up perspective. Because the Holy Spirit inspired the words, we must carefully unpack the meaning and intent of them. Use an expository dictionary/lexicon to understand how words are used in a particular context.

Read footnotes and commentaries. You can profit greatly from the scholars, theologians and experts who provide them. Use multiple sources to avoid theological bias. Take advantage of study Bibles. Consult Bible dictionaries, almanacs, handbooks and commentaries. Consider the different exegetical options. Investigate non-biblical sources (e.g. if you're studying the law, look into the ancient Mesopotamia Code of Hammurabi).

Search for Christ. Is the theme of Christ implicit or explicit in the text? Ask, "How should this text be understood as a witness concerning Christ?" Geisler explains, "The Bible is the instrument of God to convey the message of Christ and ... should be searched for the purpose of finding Christ, for '*to him all the prophets bear witness*' (Acts 10:43)."

Do it in community. The Bible should be interpreted relationally. The church (in the past and present) should be integral to the interpretive process. John Howard Yoder, American theologian and ethicist, provocatively made the point that "the text can be properly understood only when disciples are gathered together to discover what the Word has to say to their needs and concerns."

> God is more interested in how we act on His Word than in what we know about the Word

Apply, Apply, Apply! "The Bible is a message that from start to finish seeks our response," says Pauline Hoggarth, who was Scripture Union International's Bible ministries coordinator. If we fail to apply and obey the Word, we fail in our interpretation of the Word. God is more interested in how we act on His Word than in what we know about the Word. The goal should be to interpret Scripture in order to apply it with grace and mercy. In order to apply Scripture we must not only understand texts in their original frameworks, but we must also understand culture and the contexts of our lives.

An important final comment: The Bible includes uncomfortable, offensive, uncongenial or difficult passages that present unique interpretive challenges. The roles of women and men in the church, homosexuality and incest, sin and judgment, suffering and evil, predestination, genocide and war, just to name a few. When we interpret the thorny passages let's keep in mind Hoggarth's counsel that "as we engage with the 'offensive word,' we urgently need God's grace to fulfil his requirement to 'do justice, and to love kindness, and to walk humbly' with him and with our brothers and sisters in Christ (Micah 6:8)."

CONTEMPLATING

Contemplative reading ... engages the human dimension with the Word and the Spirit of God. We bring ourselves to the text: eyes, questions, circumstances, heart - all of us. We watch as we read, noticing how the reading process is shaped by the Spirit. We allow the Scripture to soak into us and reprogram our heart, changing the very concerns and ideas that control our beliefs and feelings.

James C. Wilhoit and Evan B. Howard, "Discovering Lectio Divina: Bringing Scripture into Ordinary Life."

Contemplation is actively dwelling on the Word "in the presence of God, under the eye of God, with the help of God; as a means of communion with God. Its purpose is to clear one's mental and spiritual vision ... and to let His truth make its full and proper impact on one's mind and heart," says Packer. Stated succinctly, contemplation is coming to the Word of God to know God.

Contemplation enables us to satisfy our spiritual thirst through saturating our minds with the Word and reflecting on the presence of Christ. Contemplation is not an optional spiritual discipline; it's integral to Bible engagement. That's because contemplation is essential for cultivating intimacy with Christ, enlarging our vision of Christ, and engaging with Christ in everyday life.

Lectio Divina, Latin for "divine reading," later understood as "divine lesson," is the ancient practice of contemplation. It was formulated by Benedict of Nursia (480-547) who incorporated Lectio Divina into monastic life as a doorway to Bible engagement and an aid to intimate meditative prayer.

> Contemplation is not an optional spiritual discipline; it's integral to Bible engagement.

In Lectio Divina, emphasis is placed on a slow reading of the Scripture that involves a three-fold encounter of the reader, the text and the Holy Spirit. Lectio Divina is about being shaped by the Word of God, more so than gaining information about God. For this to happen the text should be read carefully, in a way that facilitates a savouring or bathing in the text. As we bathe in the text we should rely on the Spirit of God to open our eyes, ears and heart in ways that allow God's Word to soak into us.

Prayer is the inner sanctum of Lectio Divina. Wilhoit and Howard say, "It is where reading and prayer are bound together. It is a reading that comes out of a life with God and leads into life with God."

Lectio Divina doesn't have steps like other Bible reading and reflection methods. It's a "methodless method." There are four components (lectio, meditatio, oratio, contemplatio) that make up Lectio Divina and they may happen in any order or simultaneously:

Four components of Lectio Divina

Lectio (Reading/Listening) is a slow, reverential, attentive, careful and humble reading and re-reading of the text. Lectio is listening in a spirit of silence and awe, with a deep sense of our weaknesses, in order to hear the voice of God. In Lectio we listen for a word, phrase or concept from God that speaks to us intimately and personally.

Meditatio (Meditation) is savouring, repeating, pondering, or soaking in God's Word. Through meditatio we allow God's Word to become His Word for us, a Word that touches us and affects us at our deepest levels. The Scriptural invitation to meditatio is found in the example of Mary who, reflecting on the events of Christ's birth, *"pondered them in her heart"* Luke 2:19. It's mulling over, ruminating, brooding and gnawing on the Word so that it becomes personally meaningful. And it's inviting God to interact with our thoughts, hopes, desires, memories and aspirations in order to receive God's Word in the depths of who we are.

Oratio (Prayer) is both a dialogue with God and an act of consecration. "The Word is not only the center of our listening, it is also the center of our response," says the Catholic writer Mariano Magrassi. God speaks to us through His Word and we speak back. It's repeating what God has said to us, praying any promises found in the text, thanking Him for insight or understanding, giving Him a sign of our surrender, allowing ourselves to be formed and transformed by the Word, and asking for help and healing. The Dutch priest and theologian

Henri Nouwen captured the essence of oratio when he said, "To pray means to open your hands before God."

Contemplatio (Contemplation) is putting aside our plans or agendas in order to rest and abide in the presence of Christ. Contemplatio resists the tendency to think about other things in order to take pleasure in being with God. It's an inward state of rest, a satisfied heart, a time when words are not necessary because we're tasting His grace and enjoying His loving embrace. Wilhoit and Howard succinctly summarize the practice of contemplatio saying, "In contemplation we just sit. God's Spirit is present. The text is still present. We are present. We wait in silence ... And in this being present, we are made new."

Lectio Divina can be a brief encounter with a text or something that takes place for a day, a few weeks, several months, or many years. It's also a private or communal practice.

Communal Lectio Divina

Here's an example of how a small group might practice Lectio Divina:

1. Listen to the Word of God. Everyone sits in silence for a few minutes and quietens their hearts and minds. The chosen text is read out loudly by the group facilitator. Each person listens for a word or phrase that catches their attention. Each person then says the word or phrase over and over in their mind while remaining silent for two to three minutes following the reading.

2. We ask, "How is my life touched by this word from God?" The facilitator reads the chosen text out loudly for a second time. Each person sits in silence and meditates on the question, i.e., "How is my life touched by this word from God?" After two to three minutes of silence the facilitator asks each person to briefly share the connection between the word or phrase and their life.

> Contemplatio resists the tendency to think about other things in order to take pleasure in being with God.

3. We ask, "What does God want me to do?" The facilitator reads the chosen text out loudly for a third time. Each person sits in silence and meditates on the question, i.e., on "What does God want me to do?". After 2-3 minutes of silence the facilitator asks each person to briefly share what they think God wants them to do.

4. Pray for each other. Each person asks God to give the person sitting next to them the strength to respond to what He is asking them to do. Each person prays according to what God has spoken into his/her life.

5. Contemplate God. When everyone has prayed, the group is silent, savouring God's presence and enjoying what He's done. There should be no talking or other distractions. After an appropriate time of silence the facilitator closes in prayer.

We should also note that Lectio Divina, as well as other Bible engagement practices, can be practiced by children. Ivy Beckwith, a writer and children's ministry specialist, says that when it comes to children, "we have no way of knowing what is going on in their heads as they reflect on the Bible story being read to them, but in my experience they do become engaged in the process and respond ... without silliness and sometimes with profundity. Children can do silence ... And as they practice Lectio, I believe God speaks to them through the text of Scripture in ways that are meaningful to them because that is what God desires to do."

IMAGINING

As created beings, one of our greatest treasures, perhaps the dearest fingerprint of God in us, is our ability to imagine.

Michael Card, "The Biblical Imagination."

Bible engagement is enriched through sanctified imagination. A healthy vibrant imagination is a good way to penetrate the Scriptures more holistically, i.e., allowing you to interact with the Scriptures as a living story.

Imagination is a God-given faculty. When imagination is subjected to and harnessed by God's Word, it helps us engage with the Scriptures in ways that enhance our ability to read, reflect, remember and respond to God's Word.

Imagination is the process of forming ideas, images or pictures of things that are not present to the senses. When we engage with the Scriptures using our imagination we begin to infuse our minds with the Word. *"You will keep in perfect peace those whose minds (Hebrew for 'imagination') are steadfast, because they trust in you"* Isaiah 26:3. Biblical imagination involves the working together of our minds and hearts. For biblical imagination to occur there needs to be what American singer-songwriter Michael Card calls "a bridge" between the mind and heart that comes from surrendering ourselves to God.

Imagination is closely linked to listening and faith. To engage God's Word with our imagination we must become good listeners. Good listening requires concentration, attention and belief. Professor Thomas Troeger claims that imagination is expanded through practice, for "We are attentive to what is."

Using imagination to engage with the Bible is sometimes called the Ignatian method, named after Ignatius of Loyola, the founder of the Jesuit Order in the Catholic Church. The Ignatian method (prepare, picture, ponder, pray, practice) was developed in the early 1500s. Ignatius believed that our deepest desire is to return God's love. He also trusted feelings - believing that feelings of joy, sorrow, peace and distress were important pointers on the path toward fruitful decisions and deeper union with God. Ignatius' Spiritual Disciplines are well-known and are used by Catholics and Protestants alike to deepen and enrich our spiritual lives.

Exercising sanctified imagination

What do we do in order to imagine the Scriptures? The key principles are:

- Ask God to refurbish your imagination.
- Engage sanctified visualization.
- Actively seek to see what God sees.
- Place yourself in the story, i.e., connect personally.
- Empathize with the characters, i.e., connect your emotions.
- Join the cast, i.e., walk through the story as one of the

characters.

- Understand experientially.
- Imagine the sights, sounds, smells, feels and tastes.
- Physically act out a scene.
- Be amazed.

Because the typical Protestant understanding of Christian faith majors on facts and the intellect, some Protestants are a little leery about using imagination as a means to reflect on Scripture. But imagination is not in conflict with the intellect. Rather, imagination is the partner of the intellect and both are equally important. If we neglect imagination, Bible engagement will suffer.

> If we neglect imagination, Bible engagement will suffer.

Some people are also reticent about using their imagination to reflect on Scripture because they believe the imagination is sinful. Professor Philip Collins wisely says, "Some would argue that our imagination is fallen and that we should not come to Scripture using our imagination at all, only our intellect. It is true that our imagination is fallen and that it can lead us into sin and deception. Who has not experienced a deceitful imagination? But the truth is that our intellect is also fallen and that it also can lead us into sin and deception. We must be careful with all aspects of our lives (thoughts, feelings, imagination, actions, relationships), measuring all against God's Word."

This is to say that Bible engagement would benefit greatly if sanctified imagination was part and parcel of every Christian's faith and practice. "In short, our problem is not an overactive imagination. The real threat is a lack of imagination, or an imagination stunted or misshaped by our experience. Through Scripture ... we can develop a hearty imagination that will help us believe and embody the gospel of Christ in our day," says theology professor Brandon J. O'Brien.

REFLECTING

Have you ever wondered why some of Jesus' stories seem to complicate or even obscure truth rather than clarify or simplify it? Perhaps it's that God, who knows us better than we know ourselves, is not content to speak simply to the rational intelligence, but informs us instead through imagination, intuition, wonder, and epiphany.

Luci Shaw, "Reversing Entropy."

According to the researchers and writers Greg Hawkins and Cally Parkinson, spending time reflecting on Scripture has the highest impact on personal spiritual practice. Hawkins and Parkinson catalogued the spiritual lives of 250,000 people at 1000 different churches and discovered that the primary catalyst for developing mature Christians is not Bible reading alone, it's Bible reading coupled with reflection.

Bible reading, together with reflection on the Scriptures results in strong Christians and healthy churches. According to the Willow Creek Association's Reveal survey there are 25 significant catalysts that help people grow in Christian faith. Of these catalysts, reading coupled with reflecting on Scripture outpaces the other catalysts by 75 percent. If we could choose only one thing to help us grow spiritually, reading together with reflection on Scripture, should be our number one choice.

Bible reading and reflection on the biblical text are two distinct spiritual disciplines. If you're simply using a Bible reading plan, you're not doing enough. Don't assume that Bible reading will result in reflection on Scripture. Reflection must be learned.

The practice of reflection is thoughtful and serious deliberation or musing on the Scripture text. It's tuning the mind and heart to draw near to God so that we can be refreshed with the spiritual waters for which our souls thirst. And it's asking God, in Foster's words, to "pour the living water that flows from Christ through the Bible into my dry and thirsty soul."

> Bible reading, together with reflection on the Scriptures, results in strong Christians and healthy churches.

How to reflect on Scripture

Here are 12 practical guidelines detailing how to reflect on Scripture:

1. Pause frequently. Take your time with the text. Reflection is lingering, not skimming the text. Temporarily halt on words or phrases that the Holy Spirit brings to your attention.

2. Search for emphasis. What are the words in the text that should be stressed or highlighted?

3. Unpack the language. Analyze the syntax and grammar. Verbs are usually the key to understanding the meaning of a sentence.

4. Define the meaning of key words. Use a dictionary or thesaurus to better understand nuances of meaning. Look up the Hebrew or Greek meaning of words for better comprehension.

5. Ponder what the text teaches about the Father, Son or Holy Spirit. Prayerfully ask, "Lord, where are you in this Scripture?"

6. Exercise sanctified imagination. Visualize the narrative and intuitively engage with the text by formulating in your mind what may not be evident to the senses. Billings says, "Our imaginations need rejuvenation so that we can perceive the wide, expansive drama of salvation into which God incorporates us as readers of Scripture."

7. Look for patterns. Search for repetitions, acrostic or chiastic structures (unique repetitions), literary rhythms, or poetic rhymes.

8. Be aware of yield signs. Words like "all," "every," "never," and "none" are yield signs that should slow us down and cause us to muse about what should be included or left out.

9. Contrast. Consider the opposite of what the verse says. For example, the opposite of, "*I have stored up your word in my heart, that I might not sin against you*" would be, "*I have* [not] *stored up your word in my heart,* [and now I] *sin against you.*"

10. Ask relational questions. Where do I find myself resonating with a word or resisting what the text is saying? What do my reactions to the text tell me about my relationships, attitudes or behaviours? What aspect of my life is being touched or spoken to through this text? How do I feel about what is being said?

11. Identify yourself in the text. Ask, "What is God saying to me?" and "If I was literally in the narrative, what role would I be playing?"

12. Perform it. Follow Christ. When it applies to you, intentionally live out the text you're reading. Reflection is the precursor to practically orientating our lives around God's Word. In Wesley's guidelines for reading Scripture he says we should come to the Word "with a single eye, to know the whole will of God, and a fixed resolution to do it."

Reflection on the Scriptures usually happens along with other Bible engagement practices. One can't, for example, pray, memorize, study, or journal Scripture without reflection. This is why it's critical for every Christian to learn basic Scripture reflection skills.

PRAYING

For freshness of utterance, for breath of comprehension, for elevation of thought, for intimacy of heart, there is no prayer like that which forms itself in the words and thoughts of Scripture.

J. Graham Miller, New Zealand/Australian Pastor.

When you pray, use the Bible.

Prayer, in most cases, has fallen on hard times. When a local church advertises a concert with a well-known singer, the auditorium is full. When that same church advertises a prayer meeting, only a few show up!

Why do we struggle to pray? Maybe it's because when we do pray, we pray out of the natural desires of our own hearts.

Prayer birthed in a me-centred heart does not touch the heart of God. For prayer to be effectual, we must pray what's on God's heart. And how do we know what's on God's heart? By reading and reflecting on His Word.

Bible engagement and prayer go together. To pray right, we must pray the Word. There are no shortcuts to true prayer. Prayer that moves the heart of God is prayer that's birthed, fuelled and sustained by the Word of God.

Are you praying the Bible? If not, the scope of your prayers is limited by your feelings and perspectives. And prayer rooted exclusively in an individual's experience may not be prayer at all.

Perhaps we struggle to pray because we're weak. Perhaps we don't really know what to pray or how to pray (Romans 8:26). Informed prayer comes from meditating on the Word and if we aren't reading the Bible, prayer in itself becomes tricky.

> Everything we need to pray effectively is found in the Word!

When prayer is grounded in the Word, it receives wings to fly. "For me it is absolutely essential that my prayers be guided by, saturated by, and sustained and controlled by the word of God," says Piper.

Tragically, for so many of us prayer remains earth-bound because it's tied to the fluctuating passions of the heart. For prayer to take flight, the Holy Spirit needs to pray in us and through us. This happens when we're praying the Bible.

Another reason why we struggle to pray is because our theme is so limited. We struggle to pray because it's all about us.

When Christ died on the cross for our sins and we embraced His forgiveness by faith, we died to the old self. The old you is now dead! *"Those who belong to Christ Jesus have crucified the flesh with its passions and desires,"* Galatians 5:24. Why then, do we continue to pray self-seeking requests?

Here's the good news for those wanting to grow in prayer: We cannot enlarge upon the prayer themes found in the Bible. Everything we need to pray effectively is found in the Word! The scope and depth of God's Word is beyond measure. Study the Word and you'll have more than enough content to pray without ceasing.

Often we struggle to pray because we try to go it alone with our own thoughts and aspirations. There's a place for individual prayer but not for individualistic prayer. Those who are in Christ are part of the Body of Christ. Our prayers are only tiny fragments that when put together form the prayer of the Church. And the fragments of prayer that make up the prayer of the Church are only true when they line up with the Word.

To pray selflessly - to pray the prayer of the Church - we must pray in the context of community. Prayer is effectual when we pray with one accord, in unity (Matthew 18:19). That's why we should always pray with another. And that other is Christ - the One who is the Word of God (John 1:1-2).

Prayer is stimulated by the Word and inspired by Christ. Remarkably, God's Word is something we receive and also return to God. How can this be? How can words that are not our own become our prayers? It happens by someone else praying on our behalf; by the One who is the Word interceding for us!

When we pray the Bible, we pray in the name of Christ. The Word belongs to us through Him. As we pray His Word, we pray prayers from His heart, which brings great delight to God.

Here's a final thought on why we struggle to pray: sometimes our prayers feel stale. We don't want to pray because we're tired of saying the same old things over and over again. "Prayers without variety eventually become words without meaning," says Donald S. Whitney, professor of Biblical Spirituality.

If you sometimes feel like God doesn't hear your prayers, if you lack confidence, are unsure about what to pray, would like your prayers to be more effectual, wish your mind didn't wander, and want to pray in line with God's will; then you need to be renewed and revived through praying the Scriptures.

Praying the Scriptures is using God's words to form our prayers. It's praying His Word back to Him. Specifically, praying the Scriptures is using the words, phrases or themes of a Scripture passage to guide, shape, and give language to our conversations with God. It's done by praying a Scripture text word for word as one's own prayer, by personalizing a Scripture text, or by turning our thoughts and feelings about a topic or theme of a Scripture passage into prayer.

> Praying the Scriptures is using the words, phrases or themes of a Scripture passage to guide, shape, and give language to our conversations with God.

Reading the Scriptures and praying the Scriptures should happen together. When we pray the Scriptures, we know we're in alignment with God's will. When we're in alignment with God's will, His Spirit directs and informs our prayers. Here's an example of how one might read and simultaneously pray Psalm 23 in a personalized way:

Praying Psalm 23

Scripture - *The Lord is my shepherd, I lack nothing.*
Prayer - Lord, thank you for being Jehovah-Raah, my Shepherd. Because you're my Shepherd, I don't need a thing. You intimately take care of everything. Please watch over my life and the lives of my family members today.

Scripture- *He makes me lie down in green pastures, he leads me beside quiet waters, he refreshes my soul.*

Prayer - Lord, thank you for giving me opportunities to rest. Sometimes I'm too busy for my own good and too preoccupied to see your beauty around me. Help me be still and know that you are God. Please rejuvenate me today.

Scripture - *He guides me along the right paths for his name's sake.*

Prayer - Thank you Lord for your guidance. You steer me along the path of righteousness. True to your name, you keep me on the straight and narrow road that leads to life. And you do it all for your glory.

Scripture - *Even though I walk through the darkest valley, I fear no evil, for you are with me; your rod and your staff, they comfort me.*

Prayer - Lord even in the bleakest circumstances you are by my side. What a relief to know that when I'm down, you are with me. So why am I anxious? There's no need for me to be afraid because I'm safe and secure in you.

Scripture - *You prepare a table before me in the presence of my enemies.*

Prayer - Thank you, Lord. I'm never forsaken. You faithfully provide for me, even in difficult times. It's remarkable. You serve and honour me when I should be serving and honouring you! And more, you do it in front of my enemies.

Scripture - *You anoint my head with oil; my cup overflows.*
Prayer - Who am I that you are so mindful of me? I'm blessed from the tip of my head to the soles of my feet! Thank you for not limiting your blessings: day in and day out, they keep on coming.

Scripture - *Surely your goodness and love will follow me all the days of my life, and I will dwell in the house of the Lord forever.*
Prayer - Your love is amazing! Wherever I am and wherever I go, you keep on chasing after me. You are good and your love endures forever. Today, tomorrow and throughout my life, your grace and mercy are with me. And when I leave this life you'll still be there, loving me forever. Thank you, you truly are my Shepherd. Because of your great love, I have everything I really need. Amen.

Reading the Scriptures and praying the Scriptures should be a continuous, seamless cycle. The Psalms are a great place to begin (Jesus prayed the Psalms), or simply go to a portion of Scripture you're presently reading and start praying it back to God.

MEMORIZING

Bible memorization is absolutely fundamental to spiritual formation. If I had to choose between all the disciplines of the spiritual life, I would choose Bible memorization because it is a fundamental way of filling our minds with what it needs. This book of the law shall not depart out of your mouth. That's where you need it! How does it get in your mouth? Memorization.

Dallas Willard, "Spiritual Formation in Christ for the Whole Life and Whole Person."

Bible engagement is strengthened and deepened through Scripture memorization. When we retain God's Word in our hearts it substantially informs our way of thinking and being. It also captivates our minds, enabling us to focus on Christ and His thoughts.

Now that's all well and good, but why should we memorize Scripture in the 21st century when we can simply read it on our smartphones?

Advantages of Scripture memorization

Some of the benefits to memorizing the Scriptures are:
- It strengthens our relationship with Christ (2 Corinthians 3:18).
- It helps us triumph over sin (Psalm 119:9, 11).
- It provides comfort or counsel (Romans 15:4).
- It helps us enjoy God (Psalm 119:111).
- It prepares us for sharing the Good News with others (1 Peter 3:15).
- It counteracts the pull of the world (1 John 2:15).
- It helps us grow deeper in the Word and deeper in Him (Psalm 1:1-3).

Memorizing Scripture is also an indication of an enormous commitment to God and His Word, draws us more fully into the Story, forces us to emotionally and visually step into the narrative, and builds our confidence in reading, reflecting, remembering and responding to the Word.

> When we retain God's Word in our hearts it substantially informs our way of thinking and being.

And more, Scripture memorization lodges the Word deep in our hearts so that when we're low, desperate, or profoundly spent - with little or no energy to reach out to God - then the words of Scripture surface in our minds as spontaneous, timely gifts to revive our strength and restore our faith.

So how does one memorize Scripture? Through a connection on LinkedIn, Jim Winner, I learnt this great Scripture memorization tip:

Assume the aim is to memorize John 3:16 from the NIV: *"For God so loved the world that he gave his one and only Son, that whoever believes in him shall not perish but have eternal life."*

Remove all the letters except for the first letter of each word. Include capital letters, and capitalize any that refer to God. Keep periods, commas, quotation marks and other punctuation.

F G s l t w t H g H O a o S, t w b i H s n p b h e l. J 3:16

Once you can quote the passage well, using the crutch, it's usually memorized. Now give it a try with another text ...

Scripture memorization guidelines

Here are several more Scripture memorization tips:
- Choose a version/translation that works for you.
- Begin with comprehension.
- Understand the text in its context.
- Pray for desire, discipline and dedication.
- Start out small, i.e., one verse at a time.
- Write the text on post-it notes and place them where you'll see them.
- Use index cards.
- Memorize texts by subject or topic.
- Repeat! Repeat! Repeat!
- Ask someone to do it with you.
- Sing, rap or chant it.
- Soak in it (or if you're a tea drinker like me, steep in it).
- Find idle time that you can fill with Scripture

memorization.
- Don't avoid passages that make you shake or squirm.
- Keep the goal in sight, i.e., to reflect on Christ.
- Check out LearnScripture.net or Memverse.com

Pope adds this important suggestion: "I advocate memorizing passages and books instead of scattered, disconnected verses. Memorizing passages, chapters, or entire books far exceeds the benefit of memorizing seventy-five independent verses. If one of your goals is to grow in your understanding of God, then you will get a more complete picture if you memorize verses that go together."

Now you may be feeling a little weak in the knees after Pope's suggestion. In fact, you may have been reading this chapter reluctantly because you have a mental block with Scripture memorization. The truth of the matter is that most of us don't have a mental block, we have what the author and speaker Tim LaHaye called an "ambition block." That is, we simply don't want to memorize Scripture because it's hard work.

Yes, Scripture memorization is hard work, but it pays great dividends when we do it. So don't be put off. If you can remember your address or phone number, you can memorize a Bible verse.

A final and very important reason for memorizing Scripture is so that we can serve the Lord by sharing His love with others. We hide the Word in our hearts so that we can express it through our hands. The benefit of memorization is clear: *"The word is very near you; it is in your mouth and in your heart so you may obey it"* Deuteronomy 30:14.

JOURNALING

Our imaginations have to be revamped to take in this large, immense world of God's revelation in contrast to the small, cramped, world of human "figuring out."

Eugene Peterson, "Eat This Book: A Conversation in the Art of Spiritual Reading."

One of the ways we learn to read, reflect, remember and respond to the Bible is through devotional writing, sacred doodling, or creating visual images inspired by our engagement with the Word. Journaling, also known as Bible journaling or illuminated journaling, is basically a creative, varied Bible reading and reflecting practice. It can be done directly in the margins of a Bible or in a journaling book.

Among our primary tools for growth are reflection, observation and questioning. Journaling is one of the more helpful practices for cultivating these tools. When we take our reflections, observations and questions and place them outside of us through writing, doodling or art, God can use the practice to deepen our engagement with the Word.

There are many forms of journaling that are as unique as the individuals who journal. For some people it's a written record of how their relationship with God is inspired, integrated, touched or transformed. It's a private space where they're able to write about how soaking in the Word strips away the obstacles to communion with God and helps them refocus on Him. For others it's a way to record, in creative artistic ways, how the Scriptures journey with them and help them grow in faith.

When I journal I use blank pages in a book to record my more noteworthy thoughts and insights with hand printed entries that have been inspired by my reflections on the Word. I don't write much. My thoughts are distilled and condensed, then categorized alphabetically according to headings that are dated. I've also been marking up one of my Bibles over the course of many years - underlining texts, jotting down sermon outlines I don't want to forget, or simply placing a date next to a verse to remind me of God's guidance in my life.

> When we take our reflections, observations and questions and place them outside of us through writing, doodling or art, God can use the practice to deepen our engagement with the Word.

My daughter, Christie, is far more creative in her approach. She has a special journaling Bible and she uses highlighters and custom pens to mark up, colour in, shade, or create word art (forming beautiful hand-crafted letters) that profiles the Scriptures that the Holy Spirit is highlighting in her heart and mind.

Types of journaling

There's neither a right nor a wrong way to journal. Other forms of journaling include, but are not limited to, the following:
- A form of scrapbooking.
- Notes in the margins.
- Something close to praying.
- Using water colour paints, stamps, pencils and other tools.
- Something like graffiti.
- Colourful memos.
- Using a Bible with extra wide margins for journaling.
- A record of encounters with God.
- Artwork that tells the story.
- A creative outlet that can be shared on Pinterest.
- A binder with prayers and drawings.
- A way to focus attention on the text through artistic reflection.
- Using PicMonkey, an online graphic design tool.
- Bible verses put together with photos.
- A private space to work through obstacles and meet with God.
- Scribbling with a sharpie.
- Using stickers, washi tapes and Pigma Microns.
- Connecting with online communities like "Illustrated Faith" and "Bible Journaling."

Journaling isn't about the quality of word-crafting or the splendour of the art. It's not about the outcome, it's about the process. The process is simple: pray, read and reflect on the text, figure out how to respond (words, art, other), do it, and thereby experience God and His Word in a creative way. Some people journal with the SOAP method (Scripture, Observation, Application, Prayer), and some use Lectio Divina. The method you use is secondary to finding a way to linger in the Word until you meet with God through your creative interaction with Scriptures.

Bible journaling is used by God to transform lives. Jann Gray, a blogger, says, "One of my favourite things that Bible Journaling has brought to my walk with the Lord is that the art and the words that I have placed onto the pages of my Bible have the ability to instantly bring back to my present memory the impact they had on me when I first learned them. It renews my mind! That is part of our inheritance ... as heirs we have unlimited access to our Father in Heaven ... and He loves to remind us that He chose us ... and my Journaling Bible has become an interactive love letter from Him to me ... and me to Him!"

SPOKEN WORD

The Word became flesh
And dwelt among us He came lowly
Perfectly holy
He came like a groom
On his way to the altar
To meet the bride
And for the dowry,
He had no cash
So He paid with his life

Jimmy Needham, "The Story (A Spoken Word)."

Bible engagement is multi-faceted. It includes many creative encounters with His Story.

"Spoken word," or more specifically "Christian spoken word," is a little known way for some people to interact with the Story. It's an oral form of Bible engagement utilizing free form or slam poetry. Popular with some young adults, it integrates word play, beat, reiteration, voice inflection, hip-hop, modulation, music, prose monologues, and even comedy, to present or perform the Word.

While spoken word is a form of poetry, there are four elements that differentiate it from other forms of poetry: it's written for performance, the themes are biblical, it should be challenging, and it should involve some acting.

According to an article, "Spoken Word Applied to the Word," in Premier Christianity, "The 'blessed are the underdogs' message of Jesus on the Sermon on the Mount - had it been filmed for YouTube - would certainly have gone viral. Particularly if he'd performed it in rhyme. Jesus was all about new messages in new ways - speaking from boats and atop mountains and from his friends' living rooms - and always with an epistle intended to make his congregation think about the accepted status quo."

> Bible engagement is multi-faceted. It includes many creative encounters with His Story.

Spoken word ...

- Is power poetry.
- Involves repetition that produces a "flow."
- Is rhythmic and passionate.
- Can be set against a musical background.
- Is a dramatic presentation of the Word.
- Uses words to bring an emphasis and focus to a biblical theme.
- Has a clear message that invokes a response.
- Is simple and relatable.
- Sometimes utilizes visual images.
- Is not a rigid form of poetry.
- Is not stuffy or structured.
- Does not necessarily follow grammatical rules.
- Is a creative expression of the Word.
- Can be presented in a church service, as a street drama, or in any suitable public forum.

Spoken Word is meant to be heard and performed, rather than read. Here's an example (despite what's lost by not being performed) by Christie Warren:

"Oh Taste and See"

O taste and see that the Lord is good.
Hmm … to taste
In haste
Would be a waste
Of the sweetness of His words
Or so I've heard
And see, apparently,
They're sweeter than honey
And more desirable than gold
Or so I'm told.
But if you have truly tasted of the kindness of the Lord
It'll surely strike a chord
And certainly afford
The opportunity to become
The salt of the earth.
For one cannot simply taste
And not wanna chase
Change pace
About face
Run the race
While fixing one's eyes on Jesus
And see
Literally
Undeniably
Indescribably

Unequivocally
See that He is good
No other thought will do
No other can be true
So how can we continue
To live our lives this way
When He's shifted our perspective
When everything has changed
How can we put up this facade
And play with full bravado
And silently just plod, plod, plod
Through this life?
We can't
End rant
We have to take a stand
We have to actually be
His feet and hands.
For when we taste and when we see
We're changed eternally
And I, for one, can't simply let that be
Join me?

SINGING

I can't imagine not being able to sing to God - it would be like losing a leg, or worse, having a stroke with no promise of recovery! But that isn't surprising, for praise and worship is an integral, joyful component of Christian faith (Ephesians 5:19-20).

When we sing Scripture it becomes communication, prayer, or dialogue with God. Through singing we touch the heart of God, who in turn touches our hearts. "One of the best ways to engage God is by singing the Word," says Stuart Greaves from the International House of Prayer. "When we sing the Word, it brings our heart into alignment with God's heart, with God's ways, with God's plans, and with God's personality."

How to sing Scripture

So how should singing (psalms, hymns and spiritual songs) and Bible engagement connect? Here are 10 suggestions:

1. Singing must be rooted in Scripture. The primary content of God's communications to His people is the Scriptures. That's why it's vitally important for God's Word to inform, equip and undergird our singing. Our singing can't be Spirit-led unless it's Word-fed. This is foundational and absolutely necessary. Failure to connect our singing with God's Word will distance us from the One whom the Word proclaims - Jesus Christ.

2. Singing must be directed by Scripture. The songwriter and the worship leader must take their lead from God's Word. What defines psalms, hymns and spiritual songs as distinct from other songs is that they're characterized by the guidance and light of the Scriptures. "God must speak to us before we have any liberty to speak to him. He must disclose to us who he is before we can offer him what we are in acceptable worship. The worship of God is always a response to the Word of God. Scripture wonderfully directs and enriches our worship," says Stott.

3. Singing should be experiential and formational. Singing connects our heads, hearts and hands (thinking, emotions and actions) with the Word. To sing wholeheartedly we must experience (taste, see, hear, touch, smell), indwell, engage, receive, get caught up in, and re-enact the Word.

4. Singing must be Christ-centred. When we sing we must open our hearts to the love of Christ, submit our wills to the purpose of Christ, offer our lives in adoration of Christ, and fill our minds with the Word of Christ. We should want the singing of the Word of God to infuse our lives and shape us into Christ's likeness. Bob Kauflin, the director of Sovereign Grace Music, says, "A faithful worship leader combines the Word of God with music to magnify the greatness of God in Jesus Christ."

5. Lyrics matter more than music. Music should serve the lyrics, the lyrics should feed people, and the food should be the Word of God. If we don't focus on feeding on God's Word our songs will drift into emotionalism and self-absorption. But when we feed on the Word, we move beyond ourselves and enter into the presence of God.

> Our singing can't be Spirit-led unless it's Word-fed.

6. Truth transcends tunes. Tunes should always play second fiddle to truth. We should sing songs that proclaim truth, for it's truth that transforms the mind and refreshes the spirit. Professor of worship and church history, Sam Hamstra, in part referencing Marva Dawn, says in reference to church singing: "While one worship service can never give us the whole truth ... worship planners must insist that not one worship service gives us untruth or less than truth."

7. Singing should teach us who God is. "Songs are in effect theology. They teach us who God is, what he's like, and how to relate to him. 'We are what we sing' ... That's why we want to sing God's Word," says Kauflin.

8. Singing should explain, clarify or expound Scripture. God wants to illuminate our minds and fill our hearts when we sing. Let's not be tempted to sing shallow, self-centric, biblically light songs just because we like the music. We must aim to sing songs with theologically rich content and biblically faithful lyrics.

9. Singing should be corporate in nature. While it's good for individuals to read and sing the Word privately, singing and reading the Word are best done in community. Swiss theologian Karl Barth writes, "The praise of God which finds its concrete culmination in the singing of the community is one of the indispensable basic forms of the ministry of the community."

10. Singing includes musical instruments. While singing can be unaccompanied, we should note that the Bible mentions the use of instruments to accompany and enrich our praise and worship of God (Psalm 150:3-5).

Benefits of singing the Scriptures

The benefits of singing the Scriptures are:
- It enhances our experience of God.
- It aids Scripture memorization and meditation.
- It can be a form or means to pray the Scriptures.
- Lyrics are a form of poetry and poetry helps us "feel" truth
- It's a way for us to express our hopes, joys, fears, sadness

and other emotions to God.
- It facilitates healing, spiritual alignment and transformation.
- It can be a way to exhort, encourage, impart wisdom, correct and train.

Why do we sing? At the most basic level, we sing to be changed by the Word, i.e., by the One who is the Word. The song, Ancient Words, by Lynn DeShazo captures this truth:

"Holy words long preserved
For our walk in this world.
They resound with God's own heart
Oh, let the ancient words impart.

Ancient words ever true
Changing me, changing you.
We have come with open hearts
Oh, let the ancient words impart."

PREACHING

For every text in Scripture, there is a road to the metropolis of the Scriptures, that is Christ. And my dear brother, your business is, when you get to a text, to say, "Now what is the road to Christ?" ... I have never yet found a text that had not got a road to Christ in it.

Charles Spurgeon, "Christ Precious to Believers."

I'll never forget Warren Wiersbe's intensity as he gripped my hand, stared at me through large horn-rimmed glasses, and said, "Lawson, preach the Word!" When a veteran pastor, teacher, writer and theologian clearly and compellingly counsels a course of action, you do what you're told to do! Even more so when you know the directive is the same charge Paul solemnly gave to Timothy (2 Timothy 4:1-5).

It's conservatively estimated that there are more than 40 million vocational pastors, chaplains, preachers, teachers, ministers and evangelists in the world who herald or proclaim the Word. Some are faithfully and sacrificially living up to their calling. Others are failing. For Bible engagement to thrive, what's needed is "the hard work and utter dedication of a new generation of prophetic teachers who will help people to discover Scripture as utterly relevant for life today," says university lecturer David Smith.

Preaching is a vital cog in the wheel of Bible engagement. To know the Word, people have to hear the Word. To hear the Word, someone has to proclaim the Word. *"How, then, can they call on the one they have not believed in? And how can they believe in the one of whom they have not heard? And how can they hear without someone preaching to them?"* Romans 10:14.

Preaching is unique. It's not a talk about spiritual matters. It's taking a stand with God's Word. It's allowing God, by the Holy Spirit, to speak the Word through you. It requires conviction, love, patience and endurance. And it requires a kingdom perspective – preachers must never lose sight of the fact that it's not our words, but His Word we proclaim.

> Every preacher should aim to promote confidence in, community around, and conversations about the Word.

When the divine agent works through the human conduit, variety and creativity abound. Despite the fact that different preachers deliver the Word differently, every preacher should aim to promote confidence in, community around, and conversations about the Word.

How to preach the Word

Consider the following:

Read the Scriptures every time you preach the Word. Don't cut out or shorten the reading of the Word to make more time for what you want to say. The Word of God should always be the soul of the lesson or sermon.

Public reading of the Scriptures should be done with conviction, enthusiasm, passion, fluency and expression. (See the chapter on Public Reading). Worship teams and choirs practice their singing - Scripture readers should likewise practice their reading.

God's Word is holy. Read it with reverence. At the conclusion of a public reading say something like, "Hear the Word of the Lord" or "These are the most important words you will hear today."

Be prayerful. Before you preach, ask God to address and apply the Word to your heart and life. When you preach, begin with the prayer, "Lord speak to us, we're listening" or *"May these words of my mouth and this meditation of my heart be pleasing in your sight, Lord, my Rock and my Redeemer,"* Psalm 19:14.

Preach God's Word. Don't reduce the text to the scale of your own ideas, philosophy, or personal agenda. Make every effort to weave the Scriptures through every facet of what you say. Emphasize the Scriptures by saying, "The Word says" or "In ... God says." As Quicke notes, "Biblical preaching always gives Scripture first place as God's prime way of evoking his alternative reality."

Preach the whole canon of Scripture. Don't reduce the Bible to a canon within the canon by only preaching from your favourite books, texts or stories. *"All Scripture is God-breathed* *and is useful for teaching, rebuking, correcting and training in righteousness"* 2 Timothy 3:16.

Preach all the major sub-themes of the Bible. Over the course of time your group, congregation, or class should understand the meta-narrative of creation, fall, redemption and consummation, and how, within this structure, events are still unfolding.

Major on expository or textual preaching. Methodologically speaking, expository (verse by verse through a book of the Bible) or textual (through a section of a book of the Bible) preaching should be more common than thematic (using several texts throughout the Bible) preaching because it models the importance of reading and reflecting on whole books of Scripture.

Let the Word speak for itself. The Bible's not a tool to be manipulated. Don't overshadow it with your stories, presentation style, exegetical prowess, creativity or personality. And don't detract from it by lack of preparation, personal reservations, luke-warmness, academic arrogance or intellectual presumption.

Don't try to justify or defend the Word. God's Word doesn't need to be proved, protected or preserved. It is, when all is said and done, His Word, not our word. And His Word is powerful and effective.

Never forget that it's the Holy Spirit who gives life to the Word, enabling the listener to hear the Word and live it out.

Only God can speak and sustain His Word. The preacher's role is to serve as a conduit – nothing more and nothing less.

Always remember that God's Word is far more important than anything a preacher can ever say about it. The primary aim of all preaching should be to equip others to actively indwell, engage and get caught up in receiving and reenacting the Word.

Checklist for preachers

With the above in mind, here's a brief Bible engagement checklist for preachers. Is your preaching:

- Christ-centred?
- Proclaiming the Gospel?
- Profiling the Trinity?
- Exuding grace?
- Demonstrating the Spirit's power?
- Connecting with the big Story?
- Exegeting the text?
- Explaining and interpreting culture?
- Containing sound doctrine?
- Hooking in with the audience?
- Highlighting truth?
- Honouring the biblical context?
- Challenging, warning and urging?
- Organized, clear and focused?
- Authentic, relevant and authoritative?
- Encouraging questions?
- Engaging imagination?
- Helping listeners hear from God?

- Training in righteousness?
- Equipping for good works?
- Declaring the counsel of God?
- Emphasizing faith and obedience?
- Inviting repentance?
- Moving hearers to action?
- Informing the mind, inclining the heart, guiding the will?
- Prompting discussion and application?
- Forming and transforming people in Christ?
- Reflecting how you live?
- Sending people back to the Word?

Preach the Word! "The validity of the proclamation of the Word depends solely on its content ... whether or not ... it gives expression to God's Word," says German theologian Jan Rohls. Every time you step into the pulpit, make the Word the main point, not the footnote, of your sermon. Jokes and illustrations should never overshadow the Word. Through times of convenience and inconvenience, regardless of cost or response, you have an awesome trust: to give your all to declare the message of the King. Your preaching methodology, delivery style, emotional intensity, and even your sense of humour must serve one end - to explain and proclaim God's Word. Why? Because when the Bible speaks, God speaks!

> Every time you step into the pulpit, make the Word the main point, not the footnote, of your sermon.

TEACHING

It is Christ Himself, not the Bible, who is the true Word of God. The Bible, read in the right spirit and with the guidance of good teachers, will bring us to Him.

C.S. Lewis, "Letters of C.S. Lewis."

The Bible contains its own immense and diverse teaching curriculum; one that leads us to Christ and brings us to maturity. Possibly the most important thing we should know about teaching the Bible is that the Bible, in and of itself, supplies the agenda, language and subject matter for communicating its own message. The biblical model for teaching is to help people "*see,*" "*know,*" "*consider*" and "*understand*" what "*the Lord has done*" Isaiah 41:20.

> To teach the Word one must first be immersed in the Word.

Remarkably, the Bible is a living companion in the teaching process, laying the learner open to listen and obey (Hebrews 4:12). Teachers can take heart. When they instruct others in the way of the Word, they do so knowing that they're not teaching alone!

How to teach the Word

With these encouraging thoughts ringing in our ears, here are 10 ground rules for teaching the Bible:

1. Teach if you're gifted to teach. It requires people who are spiritually gifted by God to teach God's Word in a life changing way. *"We have different gifts according to the grace given us ... if it is teaching, let him teach"* Romans 12:6-7. The gift must be nurtured and used carefully and wisely, for those *"who teach will be judged more strictly"* James 3:1.

2. Observe and interpret. Bible teacher and blogger Nicole Unice says, "The Divine is in the details." To teach the Word one must first be immersed in the Word. Teaching flows out of hours and hours of reading and re-reading the Scriptures. Through the course of reading the text the teacher must contemplate, imagine, reflect, meditate, analyze, synthesize and pray. Like the producer of a movie, the teacher must scrutinize every scene and every frame, simultaneously picturing the whole story as well as every shade and tone that comprises the story.

3. Rely totally on the Teacher. People should know that the teacher is under the authority of the text. The head Teacher is the Holy Spirit. Humans, in and of themselves, have no power to change someone's heart, even with God's Word. But with the power of the Holy Spirit working through a teacher who makes her/himself available as a channel, God's Word comes alive.

4. Be flexible. Because teachers "team-teach" with the Holy Spirit, they must be open to the fact that the wind blows where it will (John 3:8). Sticking rigidly to one's research or notes may get in the way of God leading the study of His Word. Teachers must remember their subordinate role: to be the Spirit's helper.

5. Place yourself in the other person's shoes. Enter into the world of the person or people you're teaching. Ground the teaching in their experience. Teachers must clearly instruct people in the Word in ways that intersect with who they are (age group, gender, ethnicity, level of understanding, and such). For example, if you're teaching youth, you should know what energizes and motivates them.

> The Bible, in and of itself, supplies the agenda, language and subject matter for communicating its own message.

6. Structure the lesson. All lessons, regardless of how they're taught, should capture people's attention (use visual anchors), crystallize the main idea or theme of the passage (according to the context of the Scripture and the context of the learner), interpret and explain the passage, and motivate people to respond. The lesson should always stay true to the narrative, should always profile Christ, and should always reveal the transformative power of God's Word. Mike Livingstone, American professor of medieval literature, reminds us that "teaching the Bible goes beyond using a biblical passage as a peg on which to hang good ideas ... it approaches the Bible in such a way that allows the biblical text to set the agenda and to speak for itself."

7. Unpack and explain. A text is built with words. There are many words in the Bible that aren't used in everyday life. People are sometimes unfamiliar with the meaning of words like propitiation, predestined, atonement, redeemed, sanctified, and many others. Teachers must help people understand what the words in the text mean, i.e., in the original setting when they were first said. Maybe that's why C. S. Lewis, the British essayist, academic and apologist, said that a lexicon was worth more to him than a thousand commentaries.

8. Be passionate. John Wesley, the principal founder of the Methodists, said, "When your heart is on fire, people love to watch it burn." Teachers must ask God to light up their hearts for what they're going to teach. Why? Because God uses enthusiasm for the Word to open hearts and minds to the power of the Word. The point is this, if the Word hasn't gripped the teacher, the teacher won't grip the learners. God's Word should never be taught in a half-hearted way. It's a matter of integrity. God's Word should always be taught with vim and vigour.

9. Facilitate interaction. Invite contributions and comments. Ask questions that help people wrestle with the text. Cultivate curiosity by making *"the teaching about God our Saviour attractive"* Titus 2:10. Find ways to assist people to hear the text more fully and make connections to their own lives. Christian educationalist and writer Parker Palmer says, "To teach is to create a space where obedience to truth is practiced."

10. Continue learning. A good teacher is a life-long student who constantly looks for opportunities to learn from others and go deeper into the Word. You must persist in yielding to the Book; to its message, its meaning and its Mediator.

All teaching should empower learners to engage with the Scriptures themselves. Sometimes the way the Bible is taught renders it useless. The aim should be to help people learn how to think, not to tell them what to think. If our teaching doesn't help people think critically and engage deeply with the Word themselves, then the teaching process has failed. Prolific writer and prophet A. W. Tozer pertinently reminds us that "in a very real sense no man can teach another; he can only aid him to teach himself ... What the learner contributes to the learning process is fully as important as anything contributed by the teacher. If nothing is contributed by the learner the results are useless ... Perception of ideas rather than the storing of them should be the aim of education. The mind should be an eye to see with rather than a bin to store facts in."

APPLYING

When it comes to existence, to obedience, there is always something else we have to first take care of. We live under the illusion that we must first have the interpretation right or the belief in perfect form before we can begin to live – that is, we never get around to doing what the Word says.

Søren Kierkegaard, "Provocations: Spiritual Writings of Kierkegaard."

An old rabbi once insisted that the primary body part for engaging with the Word is not the ears, it's the feet.

Once we've read the Bible, we've got to live it out. But it doesn't always work that way. Some people stuff their heads with knowledge about the Bible, but do little or nothing with it. "The single most serious problem people have with the Bible is not with lack of understanding ... but obeying it - putting it into practice," say Fee and Stuart.

What we know must become what we do. Applying the Bible is the goal of Bible engagement. If the claim to live the Bible isn't made, then all our reading, meditating, interpreting, teaching and praying the Scriptures is for naught. Writer and Bible engagement advocate Whitney T. Kuniholm says, "If we really want to understand the Bible, we'll have to do more than just take a dose of Scripture. We'll have to live it; that's the most effective Bible study method of all."

The importance of applying God's Word can't be emphasized enough. When all is said and done there's essentially one worthy response to the Word of God - do it. When we reflect on it, critique it, discuss it, preach it, learn it, interpret it, or sing it, we are only making it our Word. When we do it, then we make it His Word.

> Applying the Bible is the goal of Bible engagement.

One of my simple prayers is, "Lord, make me a living epistle for you." Why do I pray this prayer? Not because the Word is authoritative and tells me to obey it, albeit that's true, but because God's Word is sweeter than honey (Psalm 119:103) and I want others, through what I say and do, to taste and see that the Lord is good (Psalm 34:8).

At the most basic level, our beliefs must be complemented with actions. As God's Word ingrains truth in our minds and hearts, our lives must be seen to reflect God's values over our own. Peterson refers to this as reading the Scriptures "in order to live ... not to live them in consequence of reading them, but to live them as we read them."

Living the Bible as we read the Bible requires integrity, intentionality and fortitude. That's easier said than done. "People talk theoretically, conceptually, abstractly," says speaker and activist Mark Scandrette. "We do anything rather than ask, 'What is Jesus inviting me to do right now?'"

How to apply the Scriptures

So how do we live the Bible as we read it right now? How do we apply it to our lives in the power of the Holy Spirit today? Here are 10 suggestions:

1. Step out in faith. Don't hold back because you've never done what the Word says you should do (2 Corinthians 5:7). Don't second-guess the Word and don't succumb to the paralysis of analysis.

2. Receive God's Word as a message from the Lord. Obedience and love go together. Apply the Word because you love the Lord (John 14:15). Foster says, "This is the 'so what' of our Bible reading. Does it shape our spirits in love and humility? Does it lead us more fully into life with God?"

3. Stop making your own decisions. To apply what God wants you to do you must stop doing only what you want to do. In the Apocrypha it says, "Those who fear the Lord seek to please him, and those who love him are filled with his law. Those who fear the Lord prepare their hearts, and humble themselves before him" Sirach 2:15-17 (NRSV).

4. Surrender your rights to God. From the biblical point of view Christians have no intrinsic or inalienable rights (Isaiah 45:9-12). We're God's creation and our response to the Word should purely be, "What does God want of me?"

5. Don't put off for tomorrow what should be done today. Act at the right time in the right way. The psalmist says, *"I will hasten and not delay to obey your commands"* Psalm 119:60.

6. Don't be selective in applying the Word. God's Word isn't a smorgasbord from which we pick and choose what we do or do not want to eat. To believe the Bible is God's Word, yet not act on it, is a form of Christian agnosticism. We must act immediately on what we understand in the Word and grapple with the texts we don't understand until we figure out how to apply them.

7. Avoid legalism. It's a sin (e.g. Luke 11:37-52) to obey commands in order to obtain salvation, maintain salvation, attempt to gain favour with God, or try to impress people. Legalism stresses the external while ignoring the internal (Colossians 2:20-23). When we apply the Word we must first align our hearts with the Word. Ryle says, "Give first the offering of the inward man. Give your heart, your affections, and your will to God, as the first great alms which you bestow, and then all your other actions, proceeding from a right heart, are an acceptable sacrifice, and a clean offering in the sight of God."

8. Exercise discernment. The Bible isn't merely a list of dos and don'ts that we check off our list. Before we apply the Bible we must employ sound interpretation and thoughtful judgment. Different genres of Scripture will require different applications. Proverbs 31:10-31, for example, is a model or ideal, not point-by-point commands to be obeyed.

9. Balance eagerness and wisdom when you apply the Word.
Don't rush ahead and make a foolish mistake based on a partial understanding of the Word and don't hold back because of scepticism.

10. Act with what McKnight calls a "relational approach."
In this approach "our relationship to the Bible is transformed into a relationship with God who speaks to us in and through the Bible." As we listen to God "we are to love God and to love others ... live out what God calls us to live out, and discern how to live out the Story in our world today."

> To believe the Bible is God's Word, yet not act on it, is a form of Christian agnosticism.

Added to what's been said, we must know that we cannot apply the Word by ourselves. "The contents of the Bible need the work of God the Spirit for the Word to bear fruit," says Billings. It's not about trying harder. Application relies on receiving God's grace. It's not up to us to apply the Word, it's up to Christ. Bible engagement doesn't occur through "direct human effort," says Foster, "but through a relational process whereby we receive from God the power or ability to do whatever we cannot do by our own effort."

We must also make sure that when we apply the Bible, we're following Jesus. This is crucial. Christ replaced sacrifices, temples, rules, rituals and priests with Himself. The old covenant has been eclipsed by the new covenant. Religion (a return to bondage) has been trumped by a relationship with Christ (freedom from bondage). So when we apply the Bible we must do so as people who *"have been released from the law so that we serve in the new way of the Spirit, and not in the old way of the written code"* Romans 7:6.

A final word from the Word: *"Therefore everyone who hears these words of mine and puts them into practice is like a wise man who built his house on the rock. The rain came down, the streams rose, and the winds blew and beat against that house; yet it did not fall, because it had its foundation on the rock. But everyone who hears these words of mine and does not put them into practice is like a foolish man who built his house on sand. The rain came down, the streams rose, and the winds blew and beat against that house, and it fell with a great crash"* Matthew 7:24-27.

PARADIGMS

This section looks at how we help one another engage with the Bible in the different ages or stages of life. It also suggests ways to strengthen Bible engagement in the family and the church.

The way we connect with the Bible needs to be customized for different groups of people. There's no "one size fits all" with Bible engagement. Children connect with the Bible quite differently than seniors do and what works for families isn't suitable for small groups.

In the following chapters I provide Bible engagement advice for everyone. There are practical tips for parents, counsel for youth workers, guidance for young adults, direction for teachers, and if you're a pastor, the final two chapters are especially for you.

As you conclude this book, try to formulate some Bible engagement next steps. Be a Bible engagement ambassador. Read this section asking, "What does God want me to do?" It may be an action plan for how you'll help your teenage son or daughter read and reflect on God's Word every day, or it may be a strategy to help your local church better facilitate and nurture Bible engagement. Whatever it is, now is the time to do it.

CHILDREN

Many church-based children's Bible teaching programs consist of entertaining interludes that pass for religious education. The passive children sit watching puppets, skits, videos, and sleight-of-hand illusions based on the Bible, Bible stories, or Bible characters. The children may interact from time to time with what's happening onstage … or they may get up to jump around while singing songs about 'pumping it up for Jesus' … Naturally children enjoy this, but I don't believe their spiritual lives or their experience with God is enhanced through these kinds of programs. There is little interaction with adult members of the faith community or the other children. There is no opportunity to wonder about or play with the Bible story. While these programs can seem wonderfully creative and child friendly, they do little to help children meet the God of the Bible and understand how to live as God's people.

Carlos Mesters, "A Liberated Reading of the Bible."

There are about two billion children in the world. Compared to previous generations, they're unique.

Children in developed nations have fewer siblings than their parents and grandparents. They're also more relationally connected with their parents than previous generations. Most of them watch videos or play games on electronic devices every day, making them the most technically literate generation ever. Because of instant downloading and streaming, instant gratification is the norm. Oral communication trumps written communication. Today's children prefer images and voice control over typing or texting and they significantly influence the way their parents spend their money and budget their time.

Concerning Bible engagement, Lewis Foster, one of the translators of the NIV and NKJV, once said that the Bible is simple enough for a child to wade in the shallow end, yet profound enough for scholars to spend a lifetime exploring its depths. That's partly true. Children should wade in the shallow end but should also learn to swim in the deep end. That is, children should learn to study, understand and apply the Bible themselves.

Ways to help children engage with the Word

So how do we help children engage with the Word? Here are 10 considerations:

1. Invite Christ into what you're doing. For many parents the thought of having to add Bible engagement into their family routines can feel overwhelming. "What if instead of saying, 'There's no time to do more' we started saying, 'We are going to let God do more with our time,'" says pastor and blogger Christina Embree. One mother took up this challenge and began writing Scripture on post-it notes and sticking them on the bathroom mirror every morning. Now her children brush their teeth while reading God's Word!

2. Model Bible engagement. Children will do what they see their parents doing and value what their parents value. Parents and Bible teachers should be deeply engaged with God's Word as a prerequisite for teaching children how to engage with the Word. Sharing a Bible story or teaching a child a biblical principle, but not living out the truth of the story or applying the principle to our own lives is hypocrisy. This is foundational - the precepts of the Bible must inform every facet of our adult lives in a visible way. Terry Clutterham from Scripture Union says, "We will never convince our children that the Bible is refreshing, vital and full of adventure if we don't find it so, if we have never longed for God with a godly dissatisfaction and found him with the help of the Bible's pages."

> Parents and Bible teachers should be deeply engaged with God's Word as a prerequisite for teaching children how to engage with the Word.

3. Begin with the basics. Teach the major theme of the Bible (Christ) and how the sub-themes fit together. Help 4 to 8 year-olds learn how God made them (creation), loves and wants to know them (birth and death of Christ, Gospel) and has a special place prepared for them (Heaven). Teach 6 to 12 year-olds the essential stories of the Old and New Testaments and how they fit together. [Recommended - The beautifully illustrated Bible Beginners series, available from SGM Canada (ages 4 to 8). The award winning, Big Bible Challenge, available from Scripture Union (ages 6 to 12)]

4. Avoid these six mistakes:

- Don't treat the Bible like a school textbook that needs to be taught, studied and learnt. The Bible is not an instructional manual; it's God's Story.

- Don't rely on entertainment-focused approaches to the Bible. The Bible is not a dull text that needs to be creatively spiced up with fun activities.

- Don't allow secondary moral lessons to usurp the primary and secondary themes of the Scriptures. The Bible is not about rules the children should keep or examples of heroes they should follow.

- Don't promote a "feel good" theology by promising children things that the Bible neither teaches nor promises. Communicate the fact that God loves and cares for children, but don't portray Him as a divine therapist who can be called on to boost their self-esteem.

- Don't rely solely on children's "story Bibles" (books that tell the stories in the words of the storyteller but are not the Scriptures), they're an inferior replacement for the real thing.

- Don't tell children that the Bible is about them. It's not about them and what they do - it's about Christ and what He's done.

5. Use audio-visual media. While entertainment focused approaches to the Bible shouldn't predominate in how we help children connect with God's Word, there's a place for making Bible engagement fun. With thoughtfulness and care, introduce children to biblical games, dramas, films, music, apps and online resources to help facilitate a core understanding of the content of the Bible. [Recommended: Guardians of Ancora, Max7 and the Bible App for Kids]

6. Facilitate meditation on the Scriptures. Children must learn how their lives fit into God's Story. For this to happen, we need to show children how to inhabit the story by engaging their imaginations. We must aim to teach and help children contemplate and reflect on the Word for themselves.

7. Go deeper. "It's no longer enough to teach our children Bible stories; they need doctrine and apologetics," says American analytic philosopher, William Lane Craig. If the elementary schooling system can teach children to master mathematical theories and computations that many adults cannot do, then we should push the limits with our Christian children as well. Challenge them with basic theology, apologetics, doctrine, ethics and biblically related studies. But, most importantly, do so in a way that empowers them to experience and apply the Scriptures for themselves.

8. Focus on the narrative. Children intuitively understand narratives - they know how stories unfold. By connecting a passage of Scripture to the larger narrative, you can help them engage with the story of the Bible on a deeper level. Of course, the child's age and stage of development will dictate what is suitable. Be careful however not to sanitize or truncate the narrative (e.g. many older children do not know that the Christmas story includes Herod killing children under two year olds in Bethlehem). That said, wisdom dictates that we guide children to read portions of the narrative that are age-appropriate.

9. Invite and encourage questions. Our interaction with the Story needs to become their interaction with the Story. For this to happen they need the freedom to ask any and all types of questions. It's okay if we don't have all the answers. In fact it's okay for children to learn that we also struggle in understanding and applying the Bible.

10. Facilitate what theologian and child development consultant Jerome Berryman calls "Godly Play." Play is essential for developing social, emotional, cognitive and physical skills in children. It may also be the means whereby children learn the most. Use play-based activities for children to explore the significance of the narrative. Simple activities like painting or drawing a story help children imprint the narrative in their minds and hearts.

Ways to augment children's Bible engagement

There's much more that could be said about how to help children study, understand and apply the Bible themselves. For the sake of brevity, here are 20 pithy comments on ways to enhance children's engagement with the Bible:

1. Pray that your children will come alive to God's Story.

2. Show them how to use basic research tools (Bible dictionary and commentary).

3. Demonstrate how to use online resources like BibleGateway and various study apps that you use.

4. Help them listen by giving them an audio device with a downloaded audio Bible.

5. Encourage Scripture memorization.

6. Help them learn the order of the books of the Bible.

7. Learn Scripture songs together.

8. Help them handwrite verses that they can tape on their bedroom walls.

9. Give them maps so they can see where a biblical story or event happened.

10. Take advantage of teachable moments, i.e., share texts that speak to their immediate needs.

11. Help them turn their questions and comments about the Scriptures into prayer.

12. Role play how they can apply the Scriptures to everyday life.

13. Give them age appropriate Bibles that are suitable for their reading levels.

14. Encourage them to highlight or illustrate verses in their Bibles.

15. Teach the Scriptures through the use of object lessons.

16. Share personal stories about how God's Word impacts your life.

17. Make sure they hear the Gospel and not just a load of Bible stories.

18. Teach them a Bible reading method.

19. Read the Bible to them and with them. Ask them to read the Bible to you.

20. Challenge them, through involvement in practical projects and acts of compassion, to do the things they learn about in the Bible.

CENTENNIALS

How we seek to engage a post-Christian culture with the Bible needs to radically change at a global level. The practices, approaches and certainly the assumptions from just two decades ago need to be changed – and that's a real challenge for churches and mission organisations. I see the implications of Bible disengagement in that youth have no sense of how their personal story might fit into a much bigger story - God's story, as told through the Bible.

Adrian Blenkinsop, "How To Engage Young People With The Bible."

Gen Z, also known as Centennials or iGen, are those born from around 1996 to the present. Defined as "Cloud Natives," rather than "Digital Natives," they're more educated than previous generations. As they enter adulthood, the early indications are that they will be more entrepreneurial and have high hopes for making an impact in the world. They're known for being careful, hard-working, somewhat apprehensive, and concerned about the future. They cannot envision a world without smartphones, Facebook, Instagram, Twitter, Snapchat, or Tumblr. They access information instantaneously, communicate through pictures and abbreviated sentences, significantly live online, and can lose interest quickly. Their world is multi-cultural. They're safety-conscious, more private, innovative, good at multi-tasking, and are more pragmatic than other generations.

Centennials are arguably the most distracted generation of all time. Information changes daily, new technology constantly competes for their attention, interactive games are at their fingertips, and music is hardwired into their ears. For many Centennials, social media consumes them, the film industry entertains them, pornography stimulates them, and Red Bull, drugs or alcohol supercharges them.

Centennials are geared to the fast and the casual. Nothing is static. Life is measured by its cost and benefits, and there is little to no advanced planning. Selfies authenticate a young person's existence. Possibilities and options are constantly being explored and apart from school, sport, or work, structured activities are rare.

> Before we teach them the Word, we must connect them with the One who is the Word. When Centennials love the Lord, it follows that they'll love His Word.

Concerning Bible engagement with Centennials, Matt Valler from the Alchemy Project says, "The issue we are facing … is whether Christianity can find an authentic postmodern expression. Not just in style or format, but in terms of the deep structures of how we think and live. Young people are basically postmodern, the church is basically not, and therein lies the problem for the future of Bible engagement."

How to help Centennials get into the Word

So how then do we help Centennials get into the Word? Here are 20 formative suggestions:

1. Help Centennials value Christ as Lord and Saviour. Salvation is the key that opens the door to Bible engagement. It's a matter of first priorities. Unbelievers can't understand the things of the Spirit (1 Corinthians 2:11-16). Before we teach them the Word, we must connect them with the One who is the Word. Let's not put the cart before the horse. When Centennials love the Lord, it follows that they'll love His Word.

2. Teach Centennials that Bible reading is relational. When they're told they should read the Bible to know what's right and wrong, we're leading them down the garden path! First and foremost, Centennials should read the Bible to meet with God, not to inform their morality.

3. Acknowledge the difficulties. Centennials are not wired for the sustained effort required for regular Bible reading/ reflection and therefore need considerable help. Exercise patience and understanding as you teach them how to engage with the Bible.

4. Facilitate informational (analytical, critical, synthetic, inductive) and devotional (meditative, contemplative, reflective, creative) Bible reading methods. There's no single method that's ideal for every Centennial. Expose them to a broad range of methodologies and encourage them to use the Bible reading and reflecting methods they like best.

5. Cut teaching time for reading time. Help Centennials discover how to rely on the Holy Spirit to teach them truth. Prompt them to ask questions. Speak less. The more opportunities they're given to grapple with the Word and figure it out, the more they'll grow in their capacity to learn and live out the Word.

6. Push Centennials to interact dynamically with the Bible. Bible times are only quiet times (literally) for certain personality types. Engage all their senses and their imagination. Encourage them to pray the Psalms, act out Acts, grapple with Galatians, and wrestle with the Word. Help them get involved with the Scriptures both energetically and passionately.

7. Encourage routine and variety in their Bible reading. Centennials need help developing realistic and regular patterns of behaviour. They also need to change up what they're reading in the Bible (i.e., they should read from every literary genre and from both Testaments) in order to develop breadth and depth to their spirituality.

8. Connect their passions and interests to the Bible. Help them understand how their personal stories fit into God's Story. One way of doing this is to invite them to share their unrefined questions and struggles - then show them how the Scriptures provide relevant answers and guidance for their lives.

9. Encourage Centennials to read and reflect on the Scriptures with their peers and with younger children.

Confidence in the Word often grows when they're given the responsibility to help someone else read and reflect on the Bible.

10. Build accountability. Be a mentor. Personally help Centennials develop their capacity to read, reflect, remember and respond to God's Word. Check in regularly with them. Ask, "So what are you reading this week?" and "What are you hearing God say to you?" *"As iron sharpens iron, so one person sharpens another"* Proverbs 27:17.

11. Make sure Centennials are reading from a version of the Bible that's easy to read and age-appropriate. The New Living Translation and the New International Version are eminently suitable for them.

12. Provide Centennials with different entry points into the Bible. This often means helping them connect with the Bible in ways that don't require a lot of reading. For example: Manga Bible, audio versions, video/film, comic strip, or Kingstone Bible.

13. Equip Centennials with essential hermeneutical tools so they can do basic interpretation and application. The aim should be to release control of the Bible so that Centennials, adequately prepared, can engage with it themselves.

14. Introduce challenges and competitions. Centennials love to pit themselves against one another in games like Bible Jeopardy or memorization contests like the National Bible Bee.

15. Integrate technology in every possible way. Centennials are tech-savvy and techno-literate. Facilitate biblical virtual reality training. Capitalize on their addiction to digital devices. Suggest online resources that assist Bible engagement. Integrate podcasts and such into small group Bible studies.

16. Explain the benefits of Bible reading and reflection. Give compelling reasons for why they should make the effort to engage with the Scriptures.

17. Generate robust discussions about the Scriptures. Invite and encourage Centennials to ask hard, honest questions.

18. Facilitate discussion groups. Create a micro-climate for discovery and shared learning. Provide opportunities in the context of community for them to share their thoughts and insights about the Scriptures.

19. Help Centennials apply the Bible to their daily lives. Many parents and churches aren't doing this very well. Like all of us, Centennials need assistance in discerning how to live the Bible today.

20. Equip and encourage the parents of Centennials with the means, tools or resources that will help them regularly read and discuss the Scriptures with their children. The reality is that most parents leave it to ministry professionals, such as pastors and youth pastors. Create a new reality, one in which the parents become the professionals.

It should go without saying that parents, teachers and those who minister to Centennials must have a visible personal engagement with the Bible. "If the leaders of young people are not engaging with the Bible, the clear message to those they influence is that the Bible is not important," says youth Bible engagement specialist Adrian Blenkinsop. In order for adults to be visibly engaged with the Bible, they should talk about and share insights from their daily reading and reflections in the Word. They should also, in appropriate ways and at appropriate times, share their Bible engagement struggles.

Parents, teachers and leaders must also model passionate radical faith. "If Centennials lack an articulate faith, it may be because the faith we show them is too spineless to merit much in the way of conversation," says Princeton professor Kendy Casey Dean.

Of course, all of the above will lack traction if the church remains mired in modernity. While there's no magic pill for engaging Centennials with the Bible, the real work starts with the church itself. The church must get up to speed with culture. This will only happen when we step outside of our bubbles. The church must be incarnational and that means going to the places where Centennials hang out. Attractional paradigms (asking Centennials to come to the church) have limited success. There are better ways to connect with Centennials than slick programs and neatly packaged youth events. What Centennials need are open forums where the Bible is unleashed so they can genuinely explore it with their peers.

> While there's no magic pill for engaging Centennials with the Bible, the real work starts with the church itself.

MILLENNIALS

We're overwhelmed with words, and over-saturated with screens. Making the Bible an 'app' alongside News, Facebook, and email can desacralise it, potentially reducing it to simply more 'content' to be absorbed on one's device. Spiritual life may become less about "Have I heard from and spoken to and rested in God today?" and more a question of "Have I absorbed the latest reading?" Indeed in competition with the relentless 140 character outbursts available on Twitter, a lengthy reading from the Bible may seem comparatively arduous and unappealing.

Joseph Hartropp, "Apps of the Apostles: Do Millennials Read the Bible in the Digital Age?"

Millennials, also known as Generation Y or the Net Generation, are the cohort who reached adulthood in the 21st century. While there are various proposed dates for Millennials, the earliest suggested birth date is 1976 and the latest is 2004.

Millennials have grown up in a socially-networked world, are tolerant of differences, are confident and positive, rely heavily on technology, and have reasons for being optimistic yet are also anxious about their future. They can however be prone to entitlement or narcissism, and can hold unrealistic expectations that sometimes lead to disillusionment. A large percentage of Millennials are politically and religiously unaffiliated. They have more Facebook friends than any other generation, send a median of fifty texts per day, and post more selfies than other generations.

Interestingly, Millennials are also wary of institutional religion, yet are more likely than other generations to believe in the existence of a god. They are tolerant regarding sexual orientation, concerned about social justice, like to engage with good causes, and are more spiritual than religious. While Millennials tend to delay parenthood, they rate being a good parent as their top priority.

> Millennials are more open to engaging with God's Word when Bible engagement approaches begin with the questions they're asking.

How to help Millennials engage with the Bible

So how do we connect Millennials with the Bible? Here are 15 suggestions:

1. Demonstrate how methodologies work. Millennials need to know about different types of reading and reflecting methodologies before they'll use them. Exhibit Bible engagement methodologies in action and then invite them to participate.

2. Start with their life questions. Millennials are more open to engaging with God's Word when Bible engagement approaches begin with the questions they're asking.

3. Offer various choices. Millennials are consumers, they expect a range of alternatives. Provide them with a variety of Bible engagement resources, like Lectio Divina, Inductive Bible Study Method, Praying the Bible, Lectio Continua, Bible Journaling, or Spoken Word/Slam Poetry.

4. Make needs-based connections. Millennials have a penchant for social needs and world issues that revolve around injustice and compassion. Themed Bibles like God's Justice, provide a doorway to Bible reading and reflection.

5. Utilize online resources. Introduce Millennials to YouVersion, Bible Gateway, theStory and other electronic Bible engagement guides, tools and resources. Before some Millennials will use the Bible they have to be exposed to it in ways that are multi-sensory, tie in with their core values and build relational trust.

6. Cultivate small groups that value transparency, vulnerability and authenticity. Create safe places for radical honesty. When the values of Millennials are not prioritized, it's difficult to facilitate meaningful dialogue about the Scriptures.

7. Apply the Scriptures together. Millennials think in terms of community service and involvement. Link the Scriptures to practical service projects and give Millennials opportunities to serve and share what's on their hearts.

8. Read from printed Bibles. While Millennials are techno-savvy and screen-friendly, their preferred format for Bible reading is in book form.

9. Recognize that Christian Millennials have a high view of Scripture. They believe the Bible is the actual inspired Word of God, is their greatest source for moral truth, and should hold a high or the highest priority in their life of faith. In contrast, non-Christian Millennials hold ambivalent or extremely negative views about the Bible.

10. Make connections with the big screen. The majority of Millennials have seen at least one biblically-themed movie in the last year.

11. Post texts on social media. Millennials are more likely than any other generation to post and read scriptures on Twitter, Facebook, and Instagram (more than eighty per cent posted scriptures online in 2016 according to Barna).

12. Encourage the freedom to disagree. Millennials only feel safe to reveal and understand their inner selves when questions, doubts and differences are permissible.

13. Get the most out of relationships. We must live out our faith, practicing and modeling what the Bible teaches, in order for Millennials to relate. The writer Cara Meredith says, "Through belonging, Millennials not only feel known, but also find themselves further drawn to the God who no longer calls them servants, but friends (John 15:15)."

14. Use visual images. Millennials are sometimes tongue-tied when asked to interact with the written text. Try using biblically-themed visual art (e.g. paintings, wood carvings, sculptures) and asking how it links to their lives. If you then connect the art with reading or listening to the Scripture text, you can encourage Millennials to interact more openly.

15. Focus on Christ. Jesus must be the locus and agent of Bible engagement. When we invite Millennials to connect with the Word we must also invite them to connect with the One who is the Word - Jesus Christ.

Further to these suggestions, we should note that unchurched Millennials distrust metanarratives and view the church with suspicion. Bible engagement advocacy (re-establishing the Bible's relevance and credibility) is needed to help allay the fears of Millennials. This is a mammoth challenge. Confidence in the Bible has declined over many decades and it will probably take many years of collaborative efforts to reverse the decline.

ADULTS

God's Word is not something we can stand looking at from a safe distance; rather, we can (and must) take it in our hands; it touches us in our innermost being. God's Word wants to be swallowed and received in every conceivable sense. But at the same time it is no easily digestible fare, no prepared food; it must be well chewed and digested, actively consumed and interiorized. Even if at first it appears to be comprehensible and easily understandable - when we have finally taken it in, it can jolt us bitterly, destroy our inner tranquility. Its message does not leave us indifferent; rather it occupies and involves us. It can pose unpleasant questions and challenge us to action.

Claudio Ettl, "Bulletin Dei Verbum."

As Bible engagement goes, so goes the nation. When our Bibles start falling apart, society will stop falling apart.

Bible engagement impacts everything. Do we want to see sinners repent, love increase, justice triumph and righteousness prevail? Renewal begins when we read the Word for all it's worth and live it out for all to see.

Every Christian adult (18 years and older) should be soaking their hearts, minds, bodies and souls in God's Word. Bible engagement is not an option, it's a necessity. After compiling the data from a LifeWay Research study on Bible engagement, Ed Stetzer said they found this maxim to be true: "Engaging the Bible impacts one's spiritual maturity more than any other discipleship attribute." In other words, when adults feed on the Word, faith flourishes. When faith flourishes, God's kingdom grows.

If Bible engagement is essential for spiritual maturity, then why are some Christian adults not connecting with God's Word? When we're struggling to open our hearts and minds to God's Word, maybe we need to do one or more of the following:

> Bible engagement requires inclination, time and perseverance.

- Confess sin.
- Ask for forgiveness.
- Stop doing what's wrong.
- Commit fully to Christ.
- Obey Christ.
- Seek the filling of the Holy Spirit.
- Desire an encounter with God.
- Want wholeness more than brokenness.
- Pray for discipline.
- Prioritize the use of time.
- Pursue mental honesty.
- Be willing to believe and obey.
- Ask a more mature Christian to be a mentor.
- Join a Bible study small group.
- Try a different Bible engagement practice.
- Ask God to clear the way to the Word.

There are no shortcuts in reading, reflecting, remembering and responding to God's Word. Bible engagement requires inclination, time and perseverance.

Ways to personally engage with the Bible

Here are 10 practical tips for developing and deepening personal engagement with the Word:

1. Choose an appropriate version. As a rule of thumb, use a Bible that's easy to read. Keep several versions on hand for comparison and contrast. You can use an online Bible like Bible Gateway to read different versions in parallel.

2. Pray. Bible reading and reflection requires illumination from the Holy Spirit. Ask God to be your teacher. Trust Him to open your heart and mind – to give you insight and understanding (Proverbs 2:1-5). Or ask Saul's question on the Damascus road: "*Who are you Lord?*" Acts 9:5. Then read the Word, listening for the Lord's reply.

3. Use a Bible reading guide. Bible reading and reflection is enriched through the use of a reading guide. Scripture Union specializes in guides for all ages that help people deepen their understanding and grow in their relationship with Jesus.

4. Consult commentaries, lexicons and concordances. To help us read the Bible for all it's worth, we need to understand the original meaning of words, do word searches, appreciate the cultural setting of the text and learn from gifted theologians.

5. Stick to a plan. If you fail to plan, you plan to fail. Having a strategy in place or a target to aim for helps focus our connections with the Bible. A simple reading plan, while limited, is at least a way to get started and help you track your progress.

6. Mine the text. The Bible is a quarry full of precious gems. To find the gems you "dig," "crush" and "screen" the text. Don't leave a word unturned – examine it from every angle. Read and re-read until you discover the treasure. Ultimately, only Scripture can rightfully answer questions about itself.

7. Open your ears. We can listen without hearing and hear without understanding (Matthew 13:13). Sin closes our ears and dulls our spirit. Denial, pride, wrong attitudes, greed, selfish ambition, holding onto our own agenda and unforgiveness all get in the way of hearing God speak through His Word.

8. Focus on Christ. The entire Bible centres on Christ's birth, life, death, resurrection and ascension. Read the Old Testament expecting the first coming of Christ. Read the New Testament with the understanding of Christ having come and is coming back again.

9. Meditate on truth. *"Keep this Book of the Law always on your lips; meditate on it day and night, so that you may be careful to do everything written in it. Then you will be prosperous and successful"* Joshua 1:8.

10. Do it! The written Word must become the lived Word. "The basic way the Word nurtures our growth is through our obedience ... Obedience is not something I do to shape myself in God's image, but ... something I offer up so God may use it to shape me by grace," says Mulholland. So move from being hearers of the Word to doers of the Word. *"Do not merely listen to the word, and so deceive yourselves. Do what it says"* James 1:22.

Over and above what's been said, keep in mind Jesus' declaration that we *"shall not live on bread alone, but on every word that comes from the mouth of God"* Matthew 4:4. Herein lies one of the reasons for this book: Fullness of life in Christ comes from being fed by the Word. So don't short-circuit the process of reading, reflecting, remembering and responding to the Scriptures. Take every opportunity, using every means at your disposal, to feast on the Word.

SENIORS

The Bible is not an end in itself, but a means to bring men to an intimate and satisfying knowledge of God, that they may enter into Him, that they may delight in His Presence, may taste and know the inner sweetness of the very God Himself in the core and center of their hearts.

A. W. Tozer, "The Pursuit of God."

According to Abigail Trafford, a columnist for the Washington Post, a majority of people enjoy ten additional healthy years (or more) than people in previous generations. Seniors often find themselves wondering what to do with their extra time. They ask, "How do we find new ways to live and love and work at an age when our forebears would have been settling into a rocking chair?"

Every age and stage of life uniquely impacts how we connect with the Bible. As seniors engage in new ways of living and new activities, we should pay attention to the way we help seniors connect with God's Word.

How to help seniors engage the Word

Here are 10 considerations:

1. Use versions of the Bible thoughtfully. When someone's been reading a version of the Bible for many years, an affinity develops, much like a long-time friendship. If you're working one-on-one with a senior and she or he loves a particular version, then use that version. If you're working with a small group of seniors it may be wise to ask, "What version of the Bible do you like reading?" If there's consensus, use the version they want to use.

2. Discuss pertinent topics. Seniors have interests and needs that are specific to their stage of life. They're trying to figure out how to age gracefully, thrive in the empty nest, make retirement meaningful, enjoy the joys or cope with the trials of grand-parenting, deal with health problems, and prepare for death. While reading and reflection of the whole Bible should be encouraged, opportunities to explore texts that are relevant to seniors should also be facilitated.

3. Listen and learn. Some seniors are veteran Bible readers who have been feasting on the Bible for a lifetime. Their love for the Word, insights and understanding can help younger Christians grow in faith. American theologian and ethicist Stanley Hauerwas writes about how Christian communities live by memory with the old playing an essential role in the church as the keepers of the meaning; they are the repository and tellers of God's Story. So provide opportunities for seniors to teach adults, youth and children. And facilitate mentoring relationships and opportunities for seniors to interact with younger Christians (Titus 2:3).

4. Deal with competing priorities. Some seniors have very active lifestyles and may need help cultivating Bible engagement disciplines, like some of the different Bible reading methodologies. Other seniors are very lonely and inviting them to be part of a seniors Bible study group will facilitate opportunities for them to develop friendships and engage with the Bible.

5. Be aware of fatigue. As a person ages, they tire more easily. When attention span diminishes, times of Bible reading and reflecting may need to be shorter.

6. Be cognizant of physical challenges. Failing eyesight can make it hard for seniors to read the Bible, and hardness of hearing can make it difficult to hear audio Bibles. Some medications have side effects that may restrict a person's capacity to adequately read and reflect on the Bible.

7. Use large print resources. There are large print Bibles and guides that make it easier for seniors to read and reflect on the Scriptures. Some seniors who use laptops or tablets to read the Bible may need to be shown how the font size can be enlarged.

8. Equip seniors with tools and resources. Encourage seniors to share, give, or teach the Scriptures to their children, grandchildren and others. Little children, for example, enjoy having their grandparents read to them.

9. Use specialized resources. Bible reading and reflecting curriculum has been written specifically for use with people suffering from dementia, Alzheimer's or similar health issues. Tap into the range of Bible study curriculums covering topics like, "Aging in the Grace of God," "Can I Trust God With My Health," "Making Retirement Meaningful," or "Help, I'm Growing Old."

10. Be respectful. Seniors have a lifetime of experience and knowledge behind them. Maybe that's why the Scriptures say we should, *"stand up in the presence of the aged, show respect for the elderly and revere your God"* Leviticus 19:32. When we help seniors get into the Word we must do it in a way that honours them for who they are.

> When we help seniors get into the Word we must do it in a way that honours them for who they are.

And a word of counsel from Thom Rainer, president of LifeWay Resources: "As the large baby boomer generation moves into their older years, they will resist any suggestion that they are senior adults, no matter how senior they may be ... unfortunately, many churches are slow to adapt to new realities. If they do senior adult ministry the way they've always done it, it will be headed for failure."

FAMILIES

I've seen remarkable transformations take place in families. They occur when a parent does the simplest thing: picks up the Bible and reads it to the family. This is transformational because the Word of God is powerful (Hebrews 4:12; Psalm 19). When a parent does this from the sincerity of his or her heart, it always changes his or her life. It also plants the flag of Christ's authority in the center of the home.

Scott T. Brown, "A Theology of the Family."

On the human level the family is arguably the most important influence in the formation of faith. About 50 percent of all Christians are led to Christ by parents or relatives. Morality and worldview is largely fashioned by what we see and hear at home. And if parents regularly read their Bibles, pray and go to church, their children, when they become adults, are more than likely to do so as well (the converse is also true).

> The more we discuss the Bible, the more we read it - and the more we read the Bible, the more we discuss it.

Ways to get the family into the Word

Bible engagement should play a leading role in the formation of faith. Here are several practical suggestions to help get the family into the Word:

1. Use versions of the Bible that are suitable for the grade level of each member of the family. This should be a no-brainer, but some parents give their children the KJV, NRSV, RSV or NASB (versions using Grade 11 language). A child should understand what he or she is reading. Consider giving children the NIrV, NCV, TEV or NLT (versions using Grade 3 to Grade 6 language), give teens the CEB or NKJV (versions using Grade 8 language) and give young adults the ESV or NIV (versions using Grade 10 language).

2. Make it 3D. Move beyond the flat page. Utilize video, internet and other technology to augment and accentuate the stories of the Bible. The majority of 8 to 18 year-olds own cell phones, tablets, laptops or other technology. In a multimedia world it's essential for families to be able to interact with the Bible electronically. Use social media and other means to share, tweet, text or comment on a verse.

3. Have Scripture easily accessible around the home. Display favourite verses with cool prints. Hang up Scripture posters and write or paint a special text for a child or teen on the wall in her or his room.

4. Enjoy family devotionals after dinner every day. Get everyone involved. Be enthusiastic, authentic and creative. You could act out scenes in the Bible with props and costumes, pull out instruments and worship, download YouTube videos, benefit from hearty theological debates, or read Bible narratives dramatically with each characters "lines" in the story read by different members of the family.

5. Help children and teens pick out devotionals they like at a local Christian bookstore or online. Look for a devotional that unpacks the Bible with a focus on what will inform, form, conform and transform us in the way of Christ.

6. Pray and read the Bible with young children before they go to bed. There are many excellent biblical books available for young children.

7. Be seen to be reading and reflecting on the Bible. The Canadian Hemorrhaging Faith study revealed that two out of three young adults who attended church weekly as a child don't do so today. The study also revealed that when children see their parents read their Bibles, pray and go to church regularly, they are more likely to continue in the faith as adults. But when parents inconsistently or almost never read their Bibles, pray, or attend church, their children usually stop attending church just as soon as they can.

We can't conclude this chapter without recognizing a simple truth: Conversations with our families about the Bible generate Bible engagement. Research indicates that the more we discuss the Bible, the more we read it - and the more we read the Bible, the more we discuss it.

SMALL GROUPS

Many of us primarily think about engaging Scripture by ourselves during a "devotional" or "quiet time." Spending time individually with God in His Word is critical to our spiritual growth, but the Bible is clear that we are part of God's family, the church. As members of the Body of Christ, our spiritual growth is dependent on connecting with other parts of the Body – there should be no "solo" Christians. Engaging with Scripture with other believers is a key way to grow in our relationship with Christ.

Phil Collins, Taylor University Center for Scripture Engagement.

Getting together with a micro-community of believers to read and hear God's Word is an effective way to get to know God and understand how to live in a vibrant relationship with Him. In fact, research done by Collins reveals that most transformation occurs when people talk about the Bible with other people. And research done by Stetzer reveals that "through groups, people are inspired to read the Bible more, not necessarily because it's an expected duty, but because they know the joy that comes from connecting personally with God through his Word." So if you had to choose, you're better off discussing Scripture with friends than studying it alone.

How to enhance small group Bible engagement

Here are 10 ways to strengthen Bible engagement in small groups:

1. Bathe everything in prayer. Pray before, after and during the group time. When you begin, pray something like, "God, we're going to be reading your Word. Help us to engage it actively, but also to listen attentively. You are the Teacher and we're your students. Please convict, guide and transform us. Amen." For the duration of the gathering be prepared to stop the dialogue to pray the Scriptures into personal needs or situations. When you close, pray something like, "Thank you, Lord, for the way we've met with you today in and through your Word. Help us apply your Word in everything we say and do. For your honour and glory. Amen."

2. Value relationship glue. Get to know each other. Create time and space for building connections. Strong relationships are needed for heartfelt, meaningful dialogue. Foster an environment that's friendly, respectful and builds trust. Look for practical ways to love, encourage and celebrate life together (enjoying a meal together is a great way to celebrate). Respect the differences between introverts and extroverts. Ensure that everyone can share and be heard.

3. Read the Bible in multi-sensory ways. When it's apt and not gimmicky, be creative and three-dimensional; move beyond the printed page. For example, when reading about the Lord's Supper/Eucharist/Communion in 1 Corinthians 11, have a fresh loaf baking in a bread maker so that the smell pervades the air. When you finish reading the passage, eat the bread while discussing the text.

4. Teach public reading of Scripture. When we read the Bible together we should aim to read it well. Some basic instruction will help people read more confidently and meaningfully. For more information, check out the chapter on Public Reading.

5. Don't reduce the Bible to a sourcebook for finding the right answers. The purpose of a small group Bible study should never be "knowledge about the Bible." Bible knowledge isn't an end in itself, nor is it a means to an end. The aim isn't right answers; it's knowing the One who is the answer. Interact with God's Story in ways that our stories (as individuals and as a group) are formed and transformed by His Story.

> The purpose of a small group Bible study should never be "knowledge about the Bible"

6. Use open-ended questions. A facilitator should be the "guide on the side," more so than the "sage on the stage." Allowing the formulation of any answer, rather than a selection from a set of predetermined possible answers, will help people press into God's Word. Ask questions like, "What stood out for you?", "Did it raise any questions for you?", "Do you see the Father, Son or Holy Spirit in the text?", or "Why is this in the Bible?"

Avoid "duh" questions (the ones that insult our intelligence) at all costs. As a discussion progresses, direct people back into the Word. Ask, "Where do you see that in Scripture?", or "Is there something in the text that informed your perspective?" Toward the end of the discussion, ask questions that challenge them to take action.

7. Keep the Bible as the main focus. Spend more time reading the Bible than reading books, commentaries, curriculum, or study guides about the Bible. It's not a Bible study if the main activity is reading someone's book about the Bible, listening to someone preach or teach on a topic from the Bible, or watching a video series about the Bible! God's Word, read and heard, should be the primary text or content, and the Holy Spirit should be the ultimate teacher.

8. Discuss the uncomfortable and difficult passages. Be prepared to struggle with the "hard" Scriptures, even when you don't find satisfactory explanations. Wrestle with different or controversial points of view in a respectful and mature way. Facilitators should not resolve every problem or answer every question. Discussions that leave people pondering or fascinated will often lead to continued exploration of the Word. Catholic writer and theologian Thomas Merton says, "For most people, the understanding of the Bible is, and should be, a struggle: not merely to find meaning ... but to come to terms personally with the stark scandal and contradiction in the Bible itself."

9. Aim to read and hear the Scripture through the voices and ears of the whole group. Recognize how your own view of Scripture is limited, and that the fullness of Bible reading comes into its own when God speaks through different people. Be aware of how our individual personalities or denominational biases influence the way we read and hear the Scriptures. Some people are more analytical by nature, while others need to feel or experience the Word. Try to accommodate the different ways people engage with the Word.

10. Listen beyond your traditional theological grid. Allow God's Word to challenge your presuppositions. Be humble. Be aware of the limitations of your insight and understanding. Be open to how God works mysteriously and powerfully, in and through His Word, to redeem and restore your life and the lives of everyone in the group.

New Approaches

Using different methodologies may also be helpful. Try implementing one of these strategies:

The "Book Club" approach. Ask group members to read a whole book of the Bible prior to getting together, or read a big chunk when you are together (an entire story). Then open it up for dialogue. Discuss the writer's intent, themes, plot, characters, what people liked or didn't like, and so on.

The "Visual Arts" approach. Read a portion of Scripture, then view art forms (from different cultures and centuries) such as ceramics, drawings, paintings, sculptures, stained glass, wood carvings, and such, that illustrate the text. Discuss the artist's context, how she or he interprets the biblical narrative or event, and how it may or may not be true to the text.

Regardless of the strategy, in due course the teaching methodology should lead to life change. Small groups should help us become what we are called to be. A small group is ultimately successful when, according to Maria Harris an advocate for religious education, it is *"fashioning a people"* to participate in the work of God (2 Timothy 3:17).

CHURCHES

If churches could do only one thing to help people at all levels of spiritual maturity grow in their relationship with Christ, their choice is clear. They would inspire, encourage, and equip their people to read the Bible - specifically, to reflect on Scripture for meaning in their lives. The numbers say most churches are missing the mark - because only one out of five congregants reflects on Scripture every day.

Reveal Survey, Willow Creek Association.

What we say and what we do don't always line up. In October 2011, LifeWay Research conducted a study on Transformational Discipleship that included more than 4,000 American and Canadian churchgoers. The study found that while 66 per cent of churchgoers in North America say they want to "honour Jesus in all I do," only 11 per cent read the Bible daily.

Bible engagement should be intrinsic to being a disciple. "There would be no sense in saying you trusted Jesus if you would not take his advice," says Lewis. In order to learn from Christ and do what He commands, one has to read the Bible. Yet research indicates that many churchgoers rarely or never read the Bible outside of church, don't feel bad about it, and don't feel unfulfilled for not engaging with it.

Bible engagement is critical for the spiritual health and growth of the church. According to the findings of the CBES, church attendance and Bible engagement rise and fall together. The single most beneficial thing the elders, deacons, pastors, teachers or denominational leaders can do for the church is help their congregations read and reflect on the Scriptures.

> Many churchgoers rarely or never read the Bible outside of church, don't feel bad about it, and don't feel unfulfilled for not engaging with it.

Ways to nurture Bible engagement

So how can the local church better facilitate and encourage Bible engagement? Here are 10 practical suggestions:

1. Encourage everyone in the congregation to regularly read and reflect on the Scriptures.

2. Equip people with Bible reading guides, plans and resources that help them develop and sustain daily Bible reading disciplines, e.g., Scripture Union's Bible reading guides and theStory™.

3. Cultivate small groups that facilitate vigorous conversations about the Scriptures.

4. Promote, preach and teach the trustworthiness, relevance, usefulness, inspiration and uniqueness of the Bible.

5. Create opportunities or forums for people to discuss the weekly sermon and associated Scripture text.

6. Train people in public Scripture reading so that the Bible is read dynamically, clearly and compellingly.

7. Have Bibles available in the pew and actively encourage people to use them during services and gatherings.

8. Provide opportunities for people to publicly share stories and testimonies of how God strengthens, supports, comforts, inspires, informs or guides them by His Word.

9. Give everyone who doesn't have a Bible an age-appropriate, easy-to-read version (maintain a supply of Bibles, advertise availability of free Bibles).

10. Highlight the importance of Bible engagement with an annual program, quest or activity that the congregation does together, e.g., The Essential 100 Challenge.

In addition to championing Bible engagement internally (among the congregation), churches should be championing Bible engagement externally (in the world).

The most important missional task for the church today is to reach the "4/14 Window" (children between the ages of 4 and 14). Here's why: about 50 per cent of the world's population is under 20 years of age, which makes children and youth the largest group yet to be connected with Christ.

We should also be aware, based on a study by the Southern Baptist Theological Seminary, that worldwide, 71 per cent of Christians commit their lives to Christ before the age of 15 and an additional 10 per cent before the age of 19. Only 19 per cent of Christians come to faith in Christ as adults.

With the above statistics in mind, one would think that every local church would be focusing on child evangelism. But they're not. The majority of churches expend most of their money and energy on adult ministry.

Our priorities are back to front. A new focus is needed for a new era. We must wake up to the fact that each successive generation in the Western world has fewer Christians than the previous generation. It's time to act. Consideration must be given to how we can "reach, rescue, root, and release young people all over the world to grab hold of their inheritance in Christ and transform the world around them through His power," urges the Global Missions Movement.

> Bible engagement should be an essential component of any and all missional strategies to connect children and youth with Jesus.

Of course, Bible engagement should be an essential component of any and all missional strategies to connect children and youth with Jesus. If children are going to have a relationship with Christ that matters deeply, then we must do everything we can to help them acquire a deep commitment to the Scriptures.

Opening the 4/14 window.

Can we open the 4/14 window together? Developmentally-speaking, children between 8 and 12 years old are more inclined to matters of faith than at any other stage of life. For the church, this is a once-in-a-lifetime window of opportunity for the Gospel.

Jesus wants the little children to come to Him (Matthew 19:14). Imagine what could be done if the budgets of every local church were restructured to release significant financial resources to facilitate sharing the Good News about Jesus Christ with the children of the world. Then imagine what might happen if every local church incorporated Deuteronomy 6:7 into their mission statement: *"Impress them (the Scriptures) on your children."*

PASTORS

Simply teaching the Bible in church does not lead people to open the Bible for themselves throughout the week. Preaching itself isn't enough to transform deeply. God wants to work with his people individually. Our role as church leaders is to facilitate that process, to free the Bible from the confines of the pulpit and put it in people's hands.

Guy Conn, "The Big Reveal."

There are several key Bible engagement facts, gleaned from the CBES, that every pastor needs to know:

• Bible engagement and church attendance are inextricably linked.

• People who read the Scriptures a few times a week will attend church frequently.

• Local churches that major on Bible engagement are more likely to grow.

• Bible engagement is the primary factor that sustains and nourishes faith.

• Robust conversations about the Bible are strongly correlated with church health.

- Christians are built-up spiritually through conversations about the Scriptures.
- When confidence in the Bible is nurtured, church attendance is strengthened.
- If people don't have confidence in the Bible, they won't attend church.
- People who believe the Bible is relevant to life are more likely to attend church.
- People who believe the Bible is the "Word of God" are six times more likely to attend church weekly.

With the above in mind, pastors need to be very intentional about Bible engagement if they want to facilitate the health and growth of the church. This intentionality must begin with the realization that their congregations usually don't value the Scriptures in the same way they do. In fact, most Christians don't know the principles or the practices described in this book. That is, they need to be taught Bible engagement basics.

If pastors are going to facilitate the health and growth of their churches, they must plan and equip their congregations to engage with God's Word.

Plan for it. Bible engagement must permeate every facet of church ministry. Ask these questions: Does my congregation know that Bible engagement is a high priority in our church? How do they know it's a high priority in the church? Does the Sunday order of service model the priority of Bible engagement? Are the weekly small groups focusing on Bible engagement? Are children, youth, adults and seniors being taught how to engage with the Bible? Does every person in the church have a daily Bible reading guide? Do the sermons consistently remind and reinforce the importance of Bible engagement? Is Bible engagement fully integrated into the discipleship strategy of the church? How are the Scriptures used in evangelism? Is singing enriched by songs that are biblically and theologically sound? Is the Bible opened in the business meetings to inform the decision-making process? Are the finances disbursed according to the principles in God's Word? Are we supporting and praying for mission agencies that do Bible engagement ministry? How are we using our website, social media, bulletins, newsletters and PowerPoint announcements to advocate for Bible engagement? Is everything we're doing aligning with Scripture, submitting to Scripture, and seen to be subservient to Scripture?

> If pastors are going to facilitate the health and growth of their churches, they must plan and equip their congregations to engage with Gods' Word.

Inspire, encourage and equip. Pastors must teach people how to personally listen, read, pray, interpret, contemplate, study, imagine, memorize and journal God's Word, i.e., teach them Section 2 of this book. Help ministry leaders incorporate Bible engagement resources, curriculum and tools into their ministries. Discuss with the church leadership and ministry leaders how to strengthen Bible engagement with the congregations children, youth, young adults, adults and seniors. Find new ways to inject Bible engagement practices into every program and event in the church. The goal should be to make Bible engagement central to the life of the church so that people live it out as part and parcel of everything they do together.

How can pastors improve Bible engagement?

In addition to planning and equipping, there are 6 specific things that pastors should do to ramp up Bible engagement:

1. Any reading or preaching of the Word must, according to Peterson, take seriously the oral and narrative nature of the Bible. If sizeable readings of the Scripture are omitted from a church service, or only one or two verses of the Scripture are referenced in the sermon, then it's unlikely that the congregation will be shaped by the Word.

2. Focus on the Scriptures in every sermon. Preaching that doesn't major on God's Word is like a yacht without sails. If the Scriptures are only read as an appendix to what's being preached, a low view of Scripture is modeled. But when pastors find ways to demonstrate that the Scripture text(s) for the sermon are more important than what will be said about the text(s), a high view of Scripture is modeled. Furthermore, when sermons are Word-soaked, Spirit-inspired, and Christ-centred, they'll move mountains in people's hearts and minds.

3. The preaching of the Word should be exactly that; the preaching of the Word. The Bible is quite explicit on this point: *"Preach the Word ... with great patience and careful instruction,"* 2 Timothy 4:2. If the sermon doesn't focus on the Word from beginning to end, it's deficient. A sermon can be great oratory, but if it doesn't explain the Word and exegete it so that the heart of the listener is stirred to live it out, then preaching, as a component of Bible engagement, has failed.

4. Foster congregational participation and interaction with the Scriptures. Help people get meaningfully and actively involved with the Word. It's a disaster if a congregation thinks that Bible engagement is reserved for the "experts" or "professionals." Perhaps try the synagogue method from the time of Christ. That is, read the Scriptures, preach for 10 minutes, then invite dialogue by asking questions. Christianity Today writer Bret Mavrich reports that Pastor J. R. Briggs does this every Sunday. In the discussion time he asks: "What's happening in the text? What encourages or inspires me? What challenges, frustrates or offends me? What does this passage tell us about the nature of God or character of Jesus? What are we going to do about this passage in the next seven days?" The questions progress to, "What? So what? Now what?" The questions never change, yet the results are anything but predictable. "We don't merely want to fill people's head with information," Briggs says. "We want the message to run wild in our bloodstream."

5. Keep the target in mind. Paul's words to Timothy are crucial: *"All Scripture is God-breathed and is useful for teaching, rebuking, correcting and training in righteousness, SO THAT the servant of God may be thoroughly equipped for every good work"* 2 Timothy 3:16-17. McKnight says the "SO THAT" should be forcefully announced. The reason why Bible engagement is essential is SO THAT the congregation can be prepared for the jobs that God has for them. According to the Bible, the main work of the pastor isn't preaching, counselling or administering the weekly activities of the church. The main work of the pastor is to prepare *"God's people for works of service"* Ephesians 4:12. How is this done? By equipping the congregation to read, reflect, remember and respond to the Word. For when God's people are in God's Word, the Word equips them to fulfill His purposes.

6. Line up your own life with the Word. Way more is caught than taught. Congregations scrutinize everything they see the pastor say and do. Bible engagement for the pastor requires dependence on the Holy Spirit, persevering prayer, relational integrity, proclamation with humility, and grace with authority. Hoggarth reminds us that "Jesus did what he said, his life and his teaching were one integrated whole ... This coherence of teaching and life is absolutely central to the issues of effective Scripture engagement."

> When God's people are in God's Word, the Word equips them to fulfill His purposes.

All told, the challenge for pastors is "to let the Bible loose, to let it be our mouthpiece in all our debates in which we engage, to make it the substance of our proclamation and teaching, to build our own lives on its truth, in faith and obedience," says Jackman.

The fact of the matter is, Bible advocacy isn't easy. Helping a congregation grow in their engagement with the Bible is a struggle that takes a great deal of effort. Frankly, pastors need to pull out all the stops to make Bible engagement a priority in the church. When they do, they will accomplish something big, something significant, something transformational, something that advances the kingdom and brings honour and glory to God.

POSTSCRIPT

A lover who is separated from the beloved doesn't let a love letter just sit on the kitchen table unopened for days on end with the ever-growing pile of junk mail, but instead quickly and eagerly opens it upon its arrival, reading and rereading it until the ink is nearly worn off from use. Scripture is a love letter from our Divine Bridegroom ... we too should eagerly and often read the Scriptures and hear there the voice of our Beloved speaking to us.

Tim Gray, "Praying Scripture for a Change: An Introduction to Lectio Divina."

Bible engagement isn't something we master overnight. "Exposure to the contents of Scripture does not necessarily lead to a transforming encounter with God's Word," says Billings. The Bible reveals while it hides and hides while it reveals. To successfully engage the Bible with our heads, hearts and hands requires much more than reading the Scriptures, listening to sermons, or memorizing some verses.

It can be a challenge to engage with the Bible. In fact, the reality for some Christians may look like this: Commit to reading the Bible every day. Do okay for a while. Fail. Try again. Do okay for a while. Fail again. Try again. Do okay for a while. Fail again. Give up.

Maybe one of the reasons why some people fail in their efforts to read, reflect, remember and respond to God's Word is because they think it's about them; about what they need to do to please God, how they can get Him in their lives, or how to be right with Him. That's getting it back to front. Bible engagement is not about our prosperity, safety or gratification.

For others it may be that when all is said and done, Bible engagement doesn't really matter. In their heart of hearts some Christians secretly wonder if reading the Bible makes a difference. They look around and see nice people who aren't Christians and Christians who aren't nice people, and say to themselves, "Why should I read the Bible?"

When I took to the streets and asked people why they don't engage with the Bible, most people responded, "Because I don't have enough time." On the surface, this may be true. Our lives are often frenetic. But on the other hand, we're rarely too busy to surf the internet, watch television, or meet someone for a cup of tea or coffee. The truth is we think we have better things to do and we prioritize our time accordingly.

Possibly the more fundamental reason why people fail to connect with the Bible is because of sin. Some people shy away from reading the Bible because they're sustaining their lives in their own strength. Our independent spirits don't want to confess the need to be dependent on God. Pride, lack of obedience, an unwillingness to submit, and a skewed view of God result in us not doing what we should be doing.

Here's the bottom line: Bible engagement thrives when it's about Jesus, not when it's about us. "*He must become greater; I must become less*" John 3:30. We must look to Christ, and not ourselves, in order to successfully engage with the Bible. Peterson says, "One of the most urgent tasks facing the Christian community today is to counter self-sovereignty by reasserting what it means to live these Holy Scriptures from the inside out, instead of using them for our sincere and devout but still self-sovereign purposes."

And so we return to where this book started. Scripture is given to us to reveal Christ. Jesus is the theme, purpose and interpretive key to Bible engagement. He is the motive, the means and the message. Yes, Bible engagement is challenging, but it isn't complicated. Quite simply, if our relationship with Christ is healthy, our Bible engagement will be healthy.

The following story may be the best way to make this final case for Christ as the raison d'être of Bible engagement. It's a story that international evangelist Ken Terhoven, my late father-in-law, used to tell:

There was a young woman who bought a novel, read several pages, decided it was boring, threw it in a box and forgot all about it.

A year later she met a guy and fell madly in love. Some months into the relationship it was obvious they would get married. It was just a matter of time. She was waiting for him to pop the question. He was looking for a ring.

She was constantly wondering when he'd do it. Would he get down on one knee? Where would they be? Would he do it privately or publicly? She was looking for clues, gearing herself for the big event. So on the night they were enjoying a wood oven pizza at their favourite Italian restaurant she gave him her full attention when he announced, "There's something I want to tell you ... I'm a published author."

His announcement, though not what she expected, was a surprise. Why hadn't he mentioned it before? This was important. Her mind was buzzing with questions: What genre of literature did he write? How many books? Who was the publisher? Where could she buy his book?

"I'm not much of an author," he said sheepishly. "I've only written one book: a novel. It didn't sell many copies."

She sensed his pain and immediately understood why he hadn't talked about it before. He'd obviously hoped for more – maybe dreamed about the book being the launch of a successful writing career.

"What's it called?" she asked gently.

"Justice Spurned," he replied.

She was gob-smacked! That was the title of the boring novel she'd thrown in a box. What should she do? Should she say something? She wisely decided not to say anything ...

Intrigued, she was eager to get home to resurrect the book. She found it in the box behind the shoes in her closet. Pulling on her nightdress she climbed into bed, turned on the bedside light and began to read. The first paragraph captivated her. After a few pages she was spellbound. Every word was devoured, every page sent shivers up her spine. Enthralled, she read right through the night. Finally, with the first rays of sunshine poking through the chink in the curtains, she finished the book and placed it on the side-table with a contented sigh. It was the best book she'd ever read!

So what changed? Why was the book boring the first time around but riveting on the rebound? It was the same book – the same words.

Of course, we know what made the difference – we know what changed. She was head over heels in love with the author.

Similarly, when we're head over heels in love with Jesus, His Word will come alive to us. That's what love does!

PRAYER

Christ be with me, Christ within me,

Christ behind me, Christ before me,

Christ beside me, Christ to win me,

Christ to comfort and restore me,

Christ beneath me, Christ above me,

Christ in quiet, Christ in danger,

Christ in hearts of all that love me,

Christ in mouth of friend and stranger.

Saint Patrick's Lorica

RECOMMENDED RESOURCES

Blogs

American Bible Society Blog - http://news.americanbible. org/blog

Bible Gateway Blog - https://www.biblegateway.com/blog/

Bible Engagement Blog - http://www.jumpintotheword.com/

Essential Bible Blog - https://essentialbible.org/

Books

Ankerberg, John and John Weldon, *The Facts On Why You Can Believe The Bible*, ATRI Publishing, 2011.

Arthurs, Jeffery D., *Devote Yourself to the Public Reading of Scripture: Encountering the Transforming Power of the Well-Spoken Word*, Kregel Publications, 2012.

Bacote, Vincent E. Laura C. Miguélez, Dennis L. Okholm (eds.), *Evangelicals and Scripture: Tradition, Authority and Hermeneutics*, Intervarsity Press, 2004.

Barth, Karl., *Church Dogmatics, Vol 1.1: The Doctrine of the Word of God*, T&T Clark, 2010.

Bartholomew, Craig G. and Michael Goheen, *The Drama of Scripture: Finding Our Place in the Biblical Story*, Baker Academic, 2004.

Beckwith, Ivy., *Postmodern Children's Ministry: Ministry to Children in the 21st Century*, Zondervan, 2004.

Berryman, Jerome W., *Becoming Like a Child: The Curiosity of Maturity beyond the Norm*, Church Publishing, 2017.

Billings, J. Todd., *The Word of God for the People of God: An Entryway to the Theological Interpretation of Scripture*, Wm. B. Eerdmans Publishing, 2010.

Blenkinsop, Adrian., *The Bible According to Gen Z*, Bible Society Australia, 2013.

Budd, Luann., *Journal Keeping: Writing for Spiritual Growth*, Intervarsity Press, 2002.

Cross, John R., *The Stranger On The Road To Emmaus*, GoodSeed International, 2001.

Davies, Wayne., *The Forgotten Bible Reading Method: How To Read And Understand The Bible In 5 Easy Steps*, 2015.

Davis, Ellen F. and Richard B. Hayes (eds.), *The Art of Reading Scripture*, Eerdmans, 2003.

Deane, Andy., *Learn To Study The Bible: Forty Different Step By Step Methods To Help You Discover, Apply And Enjoy God's Word*, Xulon Press, 2009.

Fee, Gordon D. and Douglas Stuart, *How to Read the Bible Book by Book*, Zondervan, 2002.

Fee, Gordon D. and Douglas Stuart, *How to Read the Bible for All Its Worth*, Zondervan, 2003.

Foster, Richard J., *Life With God: Reading the Bible for Spiritual Transformation*, Harper Collins, 2010.

Geisler, Norman L., *Christ: The Theme of the Bible*, Bastion Books, 2012.

Gray, Tim., *Praying Scripture for a Change: An Introduction to Lectio Divina*, Ascension Press, 2009.

Grayston, John., *Explorer's Guide To The Bible: A Big Picture Overview*, Scripture Union, 2008.

Greene, Colin and Martin Robinson, *Metavista: Bible, Church and Mission in an Age of Imagination*, Authentic Media, 2008.

Hawkins, Greg L. and Cally Parkinson, *Move: What 1000 Churches Reveal about Spiritual Growth*, Zondervan, 2011.

Hoggarth, Pauline., *The Seed and the Soil: Engaging with the Word of God*, Global Christian Library, 2011.

Jackman, David., *Opening Up The Bible*, Scripture Union, 2006.

Jackson, Henry., *Stop Reading, Start Studying!: Inductive Bible Study Method Explained*, USA, 2015.

Kuniholm, Whitney T., *Confessions of a Guilty Bible Reader*, Scripture Union USA, 2012.

Lahaye, Tim., *How To Study the Bible For Yourself*, Harvest House Publishers, 2006.

MacArthur, John., *How To Study The Bible*, Moody Publishers, 2009.

Mathison, Keith A., *The Shape of Sola Scripture*, Canon Press, 2001.

McKnight, Scot., *The Blue Parakeet: Rethinking How You Read the Bible*, Zondervan, 2008.

McLean, Max and Warren Bird, *Unleashing the Word: Rediscovering the Public Reading of Scripture*, Zondervan, 2009.

McQuilkin, Robertson., *Understanding and Applying The Bible*, Moody Press, 1992.

Mulholland, Robert M., *Shaped by the Word: The Power of Scripture in Spiritual Formation*, Upper Room Books, 2008.

Oliver, G., *Human Bible, Holy Bible: Questions Pastoral Practice Must Ask*, Darton Longman & Todd, 2006.

Paauw, Glenn R., *Saving the Bible From Ourselves: Learning to Read and Live the Bible Well*, Inter Varsity Press, 2016.

Packer, J. I., *Truth and Power: The Place of Scripture in the Christian Life*, Harold Shaw Publishers, 1996.

Peterson, Eugene H., *Eat This Book: A Conversation in the Art of Spiritual Reading*, W. B. Eerdmans, 2006.

Pope, Janet., *His Word In My Heart: Memorizing Scripture For A Closer Walk With God*, Moody Publishers, 2013.

Quicke, Michael., *360 Degree Preaching: Hearing, Speaking and Living the Word*, Baker Academic, 2003.

Schmit, Clayton J., *Public Reading of Scripture: A Handbook*, Abingdon Press, 2002.

Smith, Christian., *The Bible Made Impossible: Why Biblicism Is Not a Truly Evangelical Reading of Scripture*, Brazos Press, 2011.

Smith, Christopher R., *The Beauty Behind the Mask: Rediscovering the Books of the Bible*, Clements Publishing, 2007.

Sproul, R. C., *Knowing Scripture*, Inter Varsity Press, 2009.

Steiner, George., *Real Presences*, Chicago Press, 1989.

Stott, John R. W., *Understanding the Bible*, Zondervan, 1999.

Strauss, Mark L., *How to Read the Bible in Changing Times: Understand and Applying God's Word Today*, Baker Books, 2011.

Sweet, Leonard and Frank Viola, *Jesus: A Theography*, W Publishing Group, 2012.

Vang, Preben and Terry Carter, *Telling God's Story: The Biblical Narrative From Beginning To End*, B7H Publishing, 2006.

Vanhoozer, Kevin J., *First Theology: God, Scripture and Hermeneutics*, Apollos, 2002.

Virkler, Henry A. and Karelynne Gerber Ayayo, *Hermeneutics: Principles and Processes of Biblical Interpretation*, Baker Publishing Group, 2007.

Walton, John H. and D. Brent Sandy, *The Lost World of Scripture: Ancient Literary Culture and Biblical Authority*, Intervarsity Press, 2013.

Warren, Rick., *Rick Warren's Bible Study Methods*, Zondervan, 2006.

Webb, William J., *Slaves, Women & Homosexuals: Exploring the Hermeneutics of Cultural Analysis*, Inter Varsity Press, 2001.

West, Robert M., *How To Study The Bible*, Barbour, 2007.

White, J. R., *Scripture Alone: Exploring the Bible's Accuracy, Authority and Authenticity* , Bethany House, 2004.

Whitney, Donald S., *Praying the Bible*, Crossway, 2015.

Wilhoit, James C. and Evan B. Howard, *Discovering Lectio Divina: Bringing Scripture into Ordinary Life*, Intervarsity Press, 2012.

Willard, Dallas., *Hearing God: Developing a Conversational Relationship with God*, Inter Varsity Press, 1999.

Wright, N. T., *Scripture and the Authority of God*, Society for Promoting Christian Knowledge, 2005.

Research

Barna - https://www.barna.com/research/

Canadian Bible Engagement Study - http://www.bibleengagementstudy.ca/

LifeWay Research - http://lifewayresearch.com/

Willow Creek Reveal Survey - https://www.willowcreek.com/move/Move_Forward_Ch1.pdf

Sites

Center for Bible Engagement -
http://www.centerforbibleengagement.org/
Forum of Bible Agencies International -
http://www.scripture-engagement.org/

Institute for Bible Reading -
http://instituteforbiblereading.org/

Taylor University Center for Scripture Engagement -
http://tucse.taylor.edu/

ORDER BIBLE
ENGAGEMENT BASICS
SCRIPTUREUNION.CA/BEB

THE AUTHOR

Lawson Murray is a Bible engagement advocate, ministry innovator, researcher, author of the bestselling children's series Bible Beginners, managing editor for the daily online Bible reading guide theStory™, culture and children's ministry consultant, conference  speaker, adjunct seminary professor, international trainer and team leader for the Canadian Bible Engagement Study. He has served as a teacher, pastor, church planter, children/youth evangelist and sports ministry specialist. His doctoral thesis focused on Bible engagement in Canada and he publishes bi-weekly articles on Bible engagement in the jumpintotheword blog.

Lawson is the President of Scripture Union Canada, a multi-media hub of resources and real life experiences connecting children, youth and families with Jesus and His Story. He is also the National Director of SGM Canada, an agency that loves to create opportunities for the Bible's life words to be shared and lived out.